Quick & Easy Recipes

Presented By
California Home Economics Teachers

Edited By
Gerry Murry Henderson

Graphics By
Laura Pierce

©*Library of Congress Catalog*
Card No. 83-072740
ISBN 0-914159-02-X

©California Cookbook Company MCMLXXXVI
116 S. Waterwheel Way, Orange, California 92669

QUICK & EASY RECIPES

"Everybody's in a hurry these days!" How many times have you heard that? It just seems to characterize today's world.

In keeping with today's life styles, everyone is rushing home from work trying to decide what they can prepare for dinner in less than 30 minutes and still carry out their evening plans. With that dilemma in mind, the California Home Economics Teachers have compiled these following recipes.

To all the recipe contributors whose names and schools appear beneath their recipes, we owe everything for the main content of this book. To the California Cookbook Company Staff, Doug Herrema, Doug Pierce, Russ Herrema, and Elaine Lazarus, each of whom have participated in the production of this cookbook, I extend a big "Thank You!" I am truly proud of the caliber of people that I get to work with! (You'll always have a "reserved parking space" with California Cookbook Company for as long as you want one; see above!)

To Laura Pierce, the Graphics Designer, I remain grateful for her many hours of creative art work.

To Gerry Murry Henderson, of Temple City High School, who procured all the color photography within this book, as well as painstakingly edited each and every recipe, I say quite candidly, "This book would never have been published without Gerry Henderson!".

Further, I express gratitude to Baskin Robbins, Best Foods, Hershey's Food Corporation, United Fresh Fruit and Vegetable Association, Pillsbury, and Lawry's who have contributed all the color photography which you will find within *Quick & Easy Recipes.*

We hope that you as the purchaser are pleased with this cookbook, and we look forward to publishing others in the years to come.

GRADY W. REED, OWNER
CALIFORNIA COOKBOOK COMPANY

CALIFORNIA HOME ECONOMICS TEACHERS ADVISORY COMMITTEE

Anderson, Jill
Santa Paula High School, Santa Paula

Benekos, George
Santiago Junior High School, Orange

Black-Eacker, Ellen
Nogales High School, La Puente

Estes, Marianne
La Mirada High School, La Mirada

Frank, Polly
Lakewood High School, Lakewood

Friederichsen, Jan
Vista Del Rio, Jr. High School, Orange

Glennan, Renee
Sequoia Jr. High School, Simi Valley

Henderson, Gerry
Temple City High School, Temple City

Hibma, Grace
Office of Los Angeles County
Superintendent of Schools, Consultant,
Consumer & Homemaking Education

Himenes, Peggy
Actis Junior High School, Bakersfield

Hsieh, Linda
Alhambra High School, Alhambra

Hulen, Donna Lyn
Los Alamitos High School,
Los Alamitos

Huntzinger, Susan
Glendale High School, Glendale

Lash, Mary
Paramount High School, Paramount

Lundy, Jeri
Grossmont High School, La Mesa

Lopez, Karen
San Luis Obispo High School
San Luis Obispo

Matsuno, Dale
Montebello Intermediate School
Montebello

Mitchell, Eudora
Norwalk High School, Norwalk

Pace, Sally
Woodlake High School, Woodlake

Pendleton, Susie
Cerritos High School, Cerritos

Phipps, Louise
Washington Middle School, Vista

Pereira, Marilyn
Hanford High School, Hanford

Priestley, Roberta
Alhambra High School, Alhambra

Pringle, Adrienne
Valley View Junior High School,
Simi Valley

Rayl, Charla
El Toro High School, El Toro

Richmond, Mary E.
San Luis Obispo High School
San Luis Obispo

Ruth, Lynda
La Mirada High School, La Mirada

Shrock, Bonnie
Kearny High School, San Diego

Traw, Marianne
Ball Junior High School, Anaheim

Wildermuth, Ellie
La Canada High School, La Canada

Wong, Pat
Taft High School, Taft

COLOR PHOTOGRAPHY CREDITS

Cover Photograph
Courtesy of Best Foods, Englewood Cliffs, New Jersey

Interior Photographs
**Courtesy of Baskin Robbins, Best Foods,
Hershey's Food Corporation, United Fresh Fruit
And Vegetable Association, Pillsbury, and Lawry's**

COLOR PHOTOGRAPHED RECIPES

TO ORDER ADDITIONAL COPIES OF "QUICK & EASY RECIPES"
Send name, address and $7.80 (includes tax and postage) to:
California Cookbook Company
116 So. Waterwheel Way, Orange, CA 92669

Other books available at $7.80 (includes tax and postage) are:

Holiday Favorites
Sweet Surprises

—CONTENTS—

* *Special Microwave Feature*

In addition to the microwave section, other recipes with microwave instructions are marked with the symbol Ⓜ.

Recipe for cover photograph, Stir-Fry Beef and Vegetables with Easy Oriental Sauce on Page 92.

Courtesy of Best Food's

Notes

Appetizers & Beverages

Artichoke Dip

Serves 6 to 8

2 cups mayonnaise
1 cup parmesan cheese
2 6 oz. jars of marinated
    artichokes, drained and chopped

1 box Triscuits or other
    crackers for serving

Mix all ingredients together except crackers, and place in a heat proof serving dish. Bake at 350° for 30 minutes. Serve immediately as a spread with crackers.

Bake in oven with main dish to conserve energy.

Linda Hsieh   **Alhambra High School, Alhambra**

Hot Beef Dip Ⓜ

Yields 2 cups

1 2½ oz. jar dried beef
1 cup cold water
½ cup parmesan cheese
¼ cup green onion, chopped

¼ cup sour cream
¼ cup mayonnaise
1 8 oz. package cream cheese
1 tablespoon dried parsley flakes

Cut beef into small pieces, using kitchen shears. Combine beef and water in 4 cup glass measure.

Microwave 4 minutes on High; drain well. Mix in remaining ingredients.

Microwave 4 to 5 minutes on Roast (7) or until hot*. Serve with crackers, vegetable sticks, chunks of bread or as a sandwich spread. Good either hot or cold.

*If your microwave has only a High setting, be sure and stir once.

This is a great make-ahead appetizer. It's colorful and a versatile dip to serve. Don't think about the calories!

Sue Nall   **Temple City High School, Temple City**

Sally's Hot Dip

Serves 8 to 10

8 oz. cream cheese
2½ oz. chipped beef
3 tablespoons onion, diced
3 tablespoons bell pepper, diced
½ pint sour cream

2 tablespoons worcestershire sauce
1 tablespoon milk
¼ teaspoon black pepper
¼ walnuts, diced
    chips or crackers

Let cream cheese come to room temperature. Dice beef, toss with onion and bell pepper. Mix cream cheese, sour cream, worcestershire, milk and pepper together until smooth. Stir beef mixture in. Place in shallow baking dish, sprinkle nuts over, cover, bake 15 minutes at 350°. Serve warm with crackers or chips.

Quick and easy; can be mixed a day ahead and baked just before serving.

George Yackey   **Santana High School, Santee**

Mexicali Dip

1 15 oz. can Hormel tamales
1 15 oz. can chili and beans
1 small onion, minced

1 4 oz. can diced Ortega
  chiles, no seeds
garlic saltto taste
1 cup cheddar cheese, shredded

Mash tamales with fork; mix well with chili and beans, onion, chili, garlic salt and ½ cup cheese. Garnish top of casserole dip with ½ cup cheese. Bake at 350° for 30 minutes. Serve with tortilla chips or Fritos.

Gloria King   *Schurr High School, Montebello*

Chili Dip Ⓜ

Serves 10 to 12

2 15 oz. cans chili con carne with beans
1 8 oz. package cream cheese
1 large package tortilla chips

Place chili con carne in a small saucepan and heat slowly. (Microwave can be used.) Cut cream cheese into slices and put them into the chili. Stir until smooth. That's it! Absolutely a hit.

Great for taking to parties. Microwave the dip for 3 to 5 minutes, and it is ready. You don't have to add anything.

Tess Osborne   *Columbus Tustin Intermediate School, Tustin*

Mexican Dip

1 16 oz. can refried beans
½ package Taco seasoning
1 8 oz. carton sour cream
3 avocados

1 package guacomole dip mix
1 8 oz. can olives, sliced
  (black, green or both)
1 medium tomato, chopped
1½ lbs. cheddar cheese, grated

Use 10 x 13 inch casserole dish. Layer ingredients. First, refried beans. Sprinkle with ½ package of Taco seasoning mix. Second, sour cream. Third, make guacomole dip mix using 3 avocados instead of 2, then sliced olives, chopped tomato and grated cheese. Serve with tortilla chips.

Great — prepare copies of this recipe. Everyone will want one.

Donna Goble   *Almondale School, Littlerock*

Joel's Easy Bean Dip

Serves 6 to 8

2 16 oz. cans Stagg's Chili Laredo without beans
1 4 oz. can diced green chilies
2 cups cheddar cheese, shredded

Mix all ingredients together in electric fondue pot, melting cheese. Serve with tortilla chips.

June Muraoka   *Cypress High School, Cypress*

Italian Dressing Dip

1 bunch green onion, chopped
1 lb. Jack Cheese, grated
2 tomatoes, chopped
1 bunch cilantro, chopped

1 4 oz. can ortega chiles, chopped
1 4 oz. can black olives, chopped
1 prepared recipe of Good Seasons
Italian Dressing Mix

Mix ingredients. Serve with tortilla chips.

Marty Thweatt   **Granite Hills High School, El Cajon**

Marsha's Crab Dip

Serves 12 to 15

1 8 oz. package cream cheese, softened
1 6 oz. can crab meat, drained and flaked
1 12 oz. bottle Home Made Chili Sauce
1 box Wheat Thins

Place softened cream cheese on a large plate or serving tray. Drain and flake crab meat and put on top. Pour chili sauce over cream cheese and crab. Dip with Wheat Thins and enjoy.

This is so quick and easy, I've used it dozens of times.

Glenell Fuller   **Glendora High School, Glendora**

Helen's Vegetable Dip

1 cup mayonnaise
1 tablespoon green onion
1 teaspoon fine herbs
½ tablespoon lemon juice
½ tablespoon worcestershire

¼ teaspoon salt
¼ teaspoon paprika
¼ teaspoon curry
1 garlic clove, crushed
½ cup whipped cream

Combine all ingredients except whipped cream. Mix well. Fold in whipped cream. Use a variety of vegetables to dip. Best to make the day before serving.

Julie Sherrill   **Dos Palos High School, Dos Palos**

Vegetable Tray With Dip

Serves 4 to 40 (depends on quantities used)

Carrots, celery, cauliflower,
green pepper, radishes,
cherry tomatoes, cucumber,
jicama, broccoli florets, etc.

Dip (may be doubled or tripled)
1 cup plain yogurt
1 cup low cal mayonnaise
1 envelope Good Seasons Dry
Cheese Italian Salad Dressing Mix
¼ cup buttermilk

Put all dip ingredients together and beat with wire whip until mixed. Set aside. Prepare all vegetables; wash, pare, trim, as needed, into bite size pieces. Arrange vegetables in an attractive pattern on a large tray with the bowl of dip in the middle. Serve immediately or cover tightly with plastic wrap and refrigerate until needed.

Carol Stewart   **Barstow High School, Barstow**

Jean's Hot Canapes

Serves 6 to 8

1 cup mayonnaise
½ cup cheddar cheese, finely shredded (mild or sharp)
1 can small or broken shrimp, drained
Optional: up to ¼ cup green onion, finely chopped
1 loaf party (petite) rye or pumpernickle bread

Combine mayonnaise, shredded cheese, shrimp and onion if used. Refrigerate if you are not going to use immediately. Before serving, arrange petite bread slices on a pan that can be used under a broiler. Place 1 tablespoon of cheese mixture on each bread round. Broil until bubbly, 2 to 3 minutes. Serve.

These may be done in the microwave, but the taste is better if broiled.

To make chili oil, used as a flavoring when stir frying or sauteeing, combine ½ cup sesame oil and ½ cup dry crushed red pepper. Warm over low heat. When warm (not hot) remove from heat, let cool and strain. Discard peppers. Store oil in glass container in refrigerator. Use sparingly until you discover correct amount to use for your taste.

Maureen Tolson   **Lompoc Valley Middle School, Lompoc**

Bacon Wraps

Yields 24

6 slices of bread   12 slices of bacon,
2 3 oz. packages of cream cheese   cut in half crosswise

Cut crusts off the bread. Set aside. Cut bread slices into four squares. Spread about one teaspoon of cream cheese over one-half of each bread square. Fold bread in half over cream cheese and wrap with one bacon slice. Secure with a toothpick. Broil until bacon is crisp. Turn frequently to prevent burning. Serve immediately.

Leftover bread crusts can be dried to make bread crumbs.

Diane Castro   **Quartz Hill High School, Quartz Hill**

Teriyaki Roll-Ups Ⓜ

Yields 50

¼ cup soy sauce   ¼ teaspoon ground ginger
1 garlic clove, minced   ¼ teaspoon salt
1 talespoon onion, minced   ½ lb. round or sirloin steak, cut
1 tablespoon sugar   diagonally into very thin strips
1 teaspoon worcestershire sauce   1 6 oz. can water chestnuts, halved

Combine soy sauce, garlic, onion, sugar, worcestershire, ginger and salt in medium mixing bowl. Add meat and stir to coat strips evenly with sauce. Marinate 30 minutes at room temperature, stirring occasionally.

Drain meat on paper towels. Wrap one strip around each water chestnut half and secure with toothpick. Arrange on shallow glass serving dish. Microwave on high for 3 to 4 minutes, rotating dish ¼ turn halfway through cooking time. Let rest 5 minutes before serving. Chill meat in freezer 30 minutes before slicing for easier handling. For variation, substitute ⅓ cup prepared teriyaki sauce mixed with garlic and onion for marinade.

Brenda Burke   *Mt. Whitney High School, Visalia*

Chutney Cheese Paté

1 small Philadelphia cream cheese, softened
1/2 cup chedder cheese, shredded
2 tablespoons sherry
1/4 teaspoon curry
1/8 teaspoon salt
1/4 cup mango chutney, finely chopped
green onions, finely chopped

Blend first 5 ingredients. Spread in a serving dish or mound in a ball shape. Chill until firm. Before serving spread with chutney and green onions. Serve with Wheat Thins.

Pat Storms   *Marysville High School, Marysville*

Seafood Cheese Ball

Serves 8 to 12

6 oz. crabmeat or shrimp
1 8 oz. package cream cheese
½ teaspoon soy sauce or more
  to taste
2 green onions, minced
dash of Tabasco sauce

Sauce

½ cup catsup
2 heaping teaspoons creamy
  horseradish
fresh parsley
crackers

Pat crabmeat or shrimp dry. Combine meat with cream cheese, soy sauce, onions, and Tabasco sauce and form into ball. Wrap in plastic and refrigerate while preparing sauce. Combine catsup and horseradish. Center seafood ball on platter and surround with fresh parsley. Pour sauce over cheese ball and arrange crackers around outer edge.

Maggie Aguirre   *Auburndale Junior High School, Corona*

Cheese Roll

Yields 2 Rolls

Velveeta Cheese
8 oz. cream cheese
7 oz. green chilies

salt to taste
chopped nuts

Soften cream cheese and Velveeta cheese separately. Roll out the Velveeta cheese between wax paper until approximately 6 x 24 inches. Combine cream cheese, chilies, and salt to taste. Spread this mixture evenly down the long side of the Velveeta cheese. Roll up and coat with chopped nuts.

Can be frozen.

Beverly Merrill   *Wangenheim Junior High School, San Diego*

Smoked Salmon Log

1 lb. can red salmon
8 oz. package cream cheese
1 tablespoon lemon juice
2 tablespoons onion, grated
1/4 teaspoon salt

1 tablespoon horseradish
1/8 to 1/4 teaspoon liquid smoke
Ingredients to roll log in:
1/2 pecans, chopped
1/4 parsley, chopped

Remove bones and skin from salmon and flake. Mix with remaining ingredients. Chill till firm. Shape into a log and roll in chopped pecan and parsley. Serve with crackers.

Freezes well.

Letitia Ponomareff   *Wangenheim Junior High School, San Diego*

Salmon Ball

Serves 12

1 lb. can red salmon
1 8 oz. pkg. cream cheese, softened
1 tablespoon lemon juice
2 teaspoons grated lemon

1 teaspoon horseradish
1/4 teaspoon hickory smoked salt
3 tablespoons fresh parsley
1 small bag pecans, minced

Pour off salmon juice and remove visible bones. Combine salmon with all ingredients, except nuts. Shape into ball. Roll in nuts and chill.

Amber Bradley   *El Capitan High School, Lakeside*

Hot Clam Dip

8 oz. cream cheese
1/4 cup white wine
1 can "Groton" chopped clams

1/4 teaspoon granulated garlic
1/4 cup chopped walnuts

Combine cream cheese and wine in a saucepan, cook over low heat, stirring constantly. Add more wine if too thick. Add chopped clams, garlic and chopped walnuts. Serve with vegetables such as green pepper, cucumbers, carrots, celery, broccoli, cauliflower, jicama, zucchini, mushrooms, etc.

Deanne Moody   *Monte Vista High School, Spring Valley*

Crab Appetizers

Serves 10 to 12 people

1 can butterflake biscuits
8 oz. cream cheese
seasoning salt

crab meat (imitation is fine)
1/2 cup cheddar cheese
1/2 cup jack sheese
dill weed flakes

Separate biscuits. Divide each biscuit into 3 parts. You will end up with 30 pieces. Put on a cookie sheet and bake for 8 to 10 minutes. Spread generously with cream cheese. Sprinkle with seasoning salt. Top with crab meat. Top with grated cheese. Sprinkle with dill weed. Bake or broil until cheese is melted.

Good for a party. They go fast. Be sure to make enough.

Jennifer Gierman   *Ball Junior High School, Anaheim*

Myron's Stuffed Mushrooms

Serves 4 to 6

20 mushrooms
3 oz package cream cheese
3 tablespoons butter

½ 4 oz. can diced green chiles
seasoned salt

Wash mushrooms, remove stems. Mound with cream cheese. Place in baking pan with butter. Sprinkle generously with diced green chiles and seasoned salt. Bake at 400° 10 to 12 minutes.

Make plenty! These disappear fast.

Lois Armstrong   *Sonora High School, La Habra*

Crab Appetizer

Yields 20

1 can water chestnuts, chopped
1 lb. crab, fresh/frozen
1 tablespoon green onion, minced

2 tablespoons soy sauce
½ cup mayonnaise

Chop the water chestnuts. Flake the crab. Mince the green onions. Mix all of the above ingredients and chill. Serve on crackers or in tiny cream puffs.

The new imitation crab works well also.

Beverly Fincher-Ranger   *Carpinteria High School, Carpinteria*

Ham Roll-Ups

Yields approximately 48

1 8 oz. package sliced ham
1 8 oz. package cream cheese, softened
4 small sweet pickles, cut in strips about ¼ inch

Separate ham slices; pat with paper towel to absorb moisture. Spread each slice thickly with the cream cheese. Place pickle strips along one edge of the ham. Starting with the pickle edge, roll up, jelly roll fashion. Cut each roll into 6 or 8 pieces. Use a cocktail toothpick to hold together.

Gloria Walker   *Casa Roble Fundamental High School, Orangevale*

"Red Onion" Nachos Ⓜ

½ to ⅓ package tortilla strips
½ cup refried beans
1 cup cheddar cheese, grated
½ can chopped green chiles, (Ortega brand)

Line an 8 to 10 inch paper plate with tortilla strips. Spread refried beans on tortilla strips (optional). Sprinkle grated cheese and top with green chiles. Place in microwave range for 2 minutes or until cheese is melted. If using broiler in conventional oven, use metal or pyrex pie plate instead of paper plate. Place nachos under broiler 1 to 2 inches from unit until cheese melts.

Lou Yergat   *Mission Viejo High School, Mission Viejo*

Popeyes

Serves 48

2 packages frozen chopped spinach
½ cup sour cream
½ cup mayonnaise
½ to 1 jar bacon bits
2 tablespoons onion soup mix
4 flour tortillas

Mix all ingredients except for tortillas. Spread the spinach mixture evenly over flour tortillas. Roll tortillas up as for a jelly roll. Chill. Cut into 1 inch slices.

Susan Roa Hope   *Lompoc Valley Middle School, Lompoc*

Banana Milk Shake

Yields 3 cups

1 cup milk
1 cup ice cubes
1 banana
2 tablespoons confectioners sugar
(or equivalent in sweetener)
½ teaspoon vanilla

Combine all ingredients in blender and blend until smooth and frothy. Serve immediately.

Dot Rhodes   *Upland High School, Upland*

Strawberry Slush

Serves 20

2 10 oz. packages sliced strawberries
2 cups daiquiri mixer
1 12 oz frozen lemonade
2 large bottles 7-UP or Squirt

Mix all ingredients together except 7-UP in a large flat pan. Freeze overnight. To serve: fill glass ¾ full of slush, add 7-UP or Squirt and mix until slushy.

Great for wedding showers. Can spike with rum/brandy!

Rita Tayenaka   *Buena Park High School, Buena Park*

Homemade Irish Cream

Serves 24

2 eggs
2 tablespoons Hersheys Chocolate Syrup
1 can sweetened condensed milk
½ pint whipping cream (not whipped)
1 cup Bushmills Irish whiskey

Beat eggs well. Add remaining ingredients and mix. Pour into bottle and refrigerate overnight. Keeps well in refrigerator at least two weeks.

Amber Bradley   *El Capitan High School, Lakeside*

Tropical Tea Warmer

12 cups boiling water
12 tea bags
⅔ cup sugar
4 tablespoons honey

3 cups orange juice
3 cups pineapple juice
2 oranges, sliced

Pour water over tea bags and let steep for 5 minutes. Remove bags. Add remaining ingredients. Cover and simmer over low heat for 2 hours or in a Crock Pot.

Marty Thweatt   *Granite Hills High School, El Cajon*

Yucca Blossoms

Serves 4

1 small can frozen limeade
Gin
2 tablespoons coconut snow
  (powdered coconut available in liquor store)
Ice cubes
1 to 2 tablespoons sugar (optional)

Put frozen limeade in blender. Save can. Add gin measured in limeade can (1 full). Add 2 tablespoons coconut snow and sugar. (If desired, drink may be prepared with no sugar.) Blend until smooth. With blender running, add 6 to 7 ice cubes, one at a time, and blend until thick and very cold.

A very refreshing drink for a summer party.

Adrienne Pringle   *Valley View Junior High School, Simi Valley*

8 Layer Dip

Serves 12

1 lb. can refried beans
salsa
jack cheese
olives

avocado
cheddar cheese
sour cream
tomato, chopped

Place these ingredients in the order given in a pan or dish. Serve with tortilla chips. (1 lb. cans work well.)

Antoinette De Neve   *Jones Junior High School, Baldwin Park*

Bread Basket Dip

1⅓ cups sour cream
1½ cups mayonnaise
2 teaspoons beau monde seasoning
2 teaspoons dill weed

2 tablespoons onion flakes,
  crushed
5 oz. dried beef, diced fine
1 loaf round bread, uncut

Mix all ingredients together. Let stand several hours in refrigerator. When ready to serve, hollow out round bread. Fill with mixture. Use bread chunks around bread and dip into mixture.

This is a recipe from one of our English teachers at school.

Jennifer Gierman   *Ball Junior High School, Anaheim*

Green Chili Cheese Quiche

Yields 60 to 70 appetizers

10 eggs
1 pint cottage cheese
1 teaspoon baking powder
1 teaspoon salt
10 drops Tabasco

½ cup flour
1 lb. Monterey Jack cheese,
  shredded
1 7 oz. can green chiles, diced
½ cup melted butter

Preheat oven to 400°F. Butter a 9x3 inch glass baking dish. In a blender mix eggs, cottage cheese, baking powder, salt, Tabasco and flour. Pour into large bowl and add all remaining ingredients. Mix well. Pour into baking dish. Bake 15 minutes at 400° then reduce heat to 350° and bake 25 to 30 minutes longer. Cut into appetizer size squares. Serve warm or cold.

This recipe is quick to prepare but takes about 45 minutes to cook. Recipe from Lawry's cookbook.

Amber Bradley   El Capitan High School, Lakeside

Delicious Tuna Paté

6½ oz. can tuna, drained
¼ teaspoon ground pepper
¼ teaspoon dried dill
8 oz. package cream cheese
  (room temperature)

2 hard cooked eggs
¼ cup chopped pistachio nuts
  (optional)

In a food processor (use a metal blade) blend in drained tuna, pepper and dill until well mixed. Add cream cheese and eggs and mix until smooth. Stir in pistachio nuts. Refrigerate overnight. Serve as a spread with crackers.

I would like to thank Marsha Norton for this great recipe.

Marianne Traw   Ball Junior High School, Anaheim

Crab Stuffed Snow Peas

Makes 60 appetizers

8 oz. package cream cheese,
  softened
1 tablespoon lemon juice
6 oz. snow crabmeat, drained

salt and pepper to taste
60 snow peas, ends trimmed
1 red pepper, cut into
  matchstick slivers

In a small bowl, mix softened cream cheese and lemon juice until smooth. Stir in crab; season with salt and pepper. Cook snow peas in boiling water for about 1 minute until wilted, but still crisp. Drain snow peas and drop into a bowl of cold water. Drain. With a sharp paring knife, split open the curved seam of each snow pea. (This may be done ahead of time.) With a small spoon, fill each snow pea with crab mixture. Garnish with red pepper.

Kathie Baczynski   Mt. Carmel High School, San Diego

Salads

Cool Strawberry Salad

Serves 6 to 8

1 large carton cottage cheese
1 large package strawberry Jello
  (or other flavor)

1 large can 20 oz. crushed
  pineapple, drained
1 12 oz. container Cool Whip

Combine cottage cheese and package of Jello. Mix well. Add drained pineapple. Fold in Cool Whip. Refrigerate over night.

Any flavor of jello may be used, selecting "color" to match occasion. Other drained fruit may be substituted.

Sally Oxford　　　　　　　　　　**Monache High Shcool, Porterville**

Lime Jello Salad

Serves 12

2 large packages lime jello
1 cup cottage cheese
2 8 oz. packages cream cheese

1 cup whipping cream
1 #2½ can crushed pineapple
greens
1 cup walnuts, chopped (optional)

Prepare jello according to the package using the pineapple juice as part of the cold water. Beat jello after it has congealed. Beat in cottage cheese, cream cheese, whipping cream, and crushed pineapple. Pour into a serving bowl or mold and refrigerate to set. Garnish with greens and serve. Optional: Add the 1 cup of chopped walnuts after adding crushed pineapple.

A great salad for all seasons and a delight with a heavy meal.

Rebecca Oppen　　　　　　　　**Dana Hills High School, Dana Point**

Strawberry Ripple Salad

Serves 8 to 10

1 large package strawberry jello
1½ cups boiling water
1 lb. 4 oz. can crushed pineapple

2 10 oz. packages frozen strawberries
2 mashed bananas
1 cup sour cream

Dissolve jello in 1½ cups boiling water. Add undrained pineapple, frozen strawberries, and bananas. Divide mixture equally and pour one part into a jello mold. Chill until firm. Spread sour cream on top and pour remaining jello mixture over the sour cream. Chill. Serve.

Rebecca Oppen　　　　　　　　**Dana Hills High School, Dana Point**

Five Cup Salad

Serves 5 or 6

1 8¾ oz. can pineapple tidbits,
  drained
1 cup drained orange segments

1 cup shredded coconut
1 cup miniature marshmallows
1 cup dairy sour cream

Combine ingredients in order given. Chill several hours or overnight.

Eudora Mitchell　　　　　　　　**Norwalk High School, Norwalk**

Pistachio Salad

Serves 6 to 8

1 box instant pistachio pudding
1 9 oz. carton whipped topping
1 16 oz. can crushed pineapple

1 cup miniature marshmallows
½ cup walnuts, chopped
¼ cup maraschino cherries,
   chopped

Fold dry pudding into whipped topping. Add crushed pineapple and juice gradually. Fold in marshmallows, walnuts and cherries. Let refrigerate until serving time.

Made in a jiffy. Terrific for potluck or family dinners.

Priscilla Bechok   **Bell Gardens High School, Bell Gardens**

Cranberry Salad

1 package red flavored gelatin
   (cherry or strawberry)
1 can cranberry sauce or
1 cup fresh diced cranberries

1 can chunk pineapple, drained
1 cup walnuts, chopped
1 cup celery, chopped
1 cup miniature marshmallows
   (optional)

Prepare gelatin according to package directions. Refrigerate until it begins to get firm. Combine the remaining ingredients. Stir and refrigerate until firm. Serve.

Great for the holidays! Easy but good!

Dixie Neal   **Granite Hills High School, El Cajon**

Easy Jello Salad

1 large package strawberry jello
1 large carton sour cream
1 large carton Cool Whip

2 small packages frozen
   strawberries
chopped walnuts

Dissolve jello, using only half the water stated on box, Refrigerate until slightly thickened. Add Cool Whip, thawed berries, sour cream, and nuts if desired. Blend thoroughly. Pour into mold and refrigerate until set.

I use ice cubes to quick set jello. Great for Christmas.

Peggy Himenes   **Actis Junior High School, Bakersfield**

Cherry Salad

Serves 12

1 can sweetened condensed milk
1 can cherry pie filling

1 small can crushed pineapple
1 small carton Cool Whip

Place first 3 ingredients in bowl and mix thoroughly. Fold in Cool Whip. Refrigerate or eat immediately.

Delicious and rich!

Donna Kinney   **Laguna Junior High School, San Luis Obispo**

Sunshine Salad

Serves 4 to 6

½ lb. longhorn (Colby) cheese, cubed
16 marshmallows, cut in pieces
1 large can pineapple chunks, drained

Dressing

1 cup pineapple juice and water
2 to 3 tablespoons sugar
1 egg, beaten
1 teaspoon vinegar
1 tablespoon cornstarch

Mix together the cubed cheese, pineapple chunks and marshmallows. Combine all ingredients for dressing and cook until it boils. Allow to boil for 1 minute.

Barbara Coddington   *Dinuba High School, Dinuba*

Date Salad

1 pint whipping cream
¼ teaspoon vanilla
1 8 oz. package cream cheese, softened
1 tablespoon honey

1 cup unsweetened pineapple, crushed and drained
1 to 1½ cups dates, chopped
1 to 1½ cups walnuts, chopped

Whip cream with electric mixer until very thick peaks. Add vanilla and softened cream cheese, blend into whipped cream mixture. Add honey to drained pineapple. Mix pineapple, dates and walnuts into whipped creamed mixture.

Dixie Neal   *Granite Hills High School, El Cajon*

Quick Pea Salad

Serves 4 to 6

½ cup crisp bacon crumbs
1 package frozen peas

½ cup green onions, sliced
¼ cup mayonnaise

Cook bacon bits until crisp in skillet or microwave. Cook peas until tender; drain. (Or cook in microwave at high temperature for 4 to 6 minutes.) Combine peas, bacon, green onions. and mayonnaise. May be served hot or cold.

Barbara Coddington   *Dinuba High School, Dinuba*

Layered Lettuce Salad

Serves 6 to 8

1 head lettuce, torn into pieces
½ cup celery, chopped
1 cup green pepper, chopped
½ cup onion, chopped
1 package unthawed frozen peas

2 cups mayonnaise
2 tablespoons sugar
4 oz. cheddar cheese, grated
½ jar bacon bits

Layer first 5 ingredients in 9x13 inch pan. Spread mayonnaise over the layers. Sprinkle with 2 tablespoons sugar. Add the cheese and bacon bits over that layer. Refrigerate overnight.

Barbara Coddington   *Dinuba High School, Dinuba*

Best Cole Slaw

Serves 6 to 8

1 head cabbage, shredded
1 cup carrots, grated
1/2 cup green pepper, diced
1 tablespoon onion, grated

salt and pepper to taste
1/4 cup sugar
1/4 cup lemon juice
3/4 cup mayonnaise

Mix shredded cabbage, carrots, green pepper and onion. Add salt and pepper. Mix together the sugar, lemon juice and mayonnaise and add to the cabbage mixture. Chill and serve.

Bonnie Parks   *Big Pine High School, Big Pine*

A Different Cole Slaw

Serves 6 to 10

1/2 to 1 head cabbage, sliced
3 to 4 green onions, chopped
2 tablespoons toasted sesame seeds
1/2 cup slivered almonds
1 package Top Ramen noodle soup
   (chicken flavor), broken up

Dressing:

3 tablespoons red wine vinegar
2 tablespoons sugar
1 teaspoon salt
1/4 teaspoon pepper
flavor packet from Top Ramen
1/2 cup salad oil

Make dressing. Combine salad ingredients adding noodles last. Serve immediately.

Sandra French   *Long Beach Unified School District*

Layered Spinach Salad

Serves 8

3 slices bacon, crisply cooked and crumbled
1 10 oz. package frozen peas (cooked until tender)
1/2 cup plus 2 tablespoons Romano cheese, grated
1 1/2 quarts fresh spinach (torn)
2 cups sliced fresh mushrooms
1 cup red onion rings
1/2 cup mayonnaise
1/2 cup sour cream
1 teaspoon sugar

In microwave cook bacon until crisp, then crumble. Cook peas in microwave until just tender. Combine 1/2 cup grated Romano cheese with bacon and mix well. In large bowl, layer: spinach, cheese mixture, mushrooms, onions and peas. Combine mayonnaise, sour cream and sugar. Mix well. Spread mayonnaise mixture over salad to seal. Sprinkle 2 tablespoons cheese over top. Cover and refrigerate overnight.

This is a good dish to take to a potluck!

Adrienne Pringle   *Valley View Junior High School, Simi Valley*

Tossed Green Salad
with Creamy French Dressing

Serves 6 to 8

8 cups torn salad greens
2 cups tomatoes, chopped
½ cup cucumber, chopped

4 tablespoons green peppers,
    chopped (if desired)
1 cup Creamy French Dressing*

In medium bowl combine salad greens, tomato, cucumber and green pepper. Pour dressing on top. Toss to coat evenly.

*Creamy French Dressing

1 cup catsup
1 cup mayonnaise or
miracle whip salad dressing
½ cup vinegar
½ cup sugar
1 teaspoon worcestershire sauce

1 teaspoon onion salt
½ to 1 teaspoon garlic salt
    (to taste)
1 cup salad oil
3 to 4 drops tabasco sauce
pepper to taste

Mix first seven ingredients until well blended. Pour into a quart jar. Add salad oil, tabasco sauce and pepper. Shake until smooth. Dressing is ready to use. Store remainder in refrigerator for future use. One tablespoon grated onion may be substituted for onion salt and a garlic clove (peeled and partially cut) may be substituted for the garlic salt. Leave garlic clove in dressing to add and flavor.

Marguerite S. Darnall   *Corona Senior High School, Corona*

Bibb Lettuce with Cream Dressing

Serves 4

1 egg yolk
⅓ cup heavy cream
1 teaspoon tarragon vinegar
¼ teaspoon salt

1/8 teaspoon ground pepper
2 small heads Bibb lettuce
2 tablespoons chives, minced
(for garnish)

In a small mixing bowl, combine the egg yolk, cream, vinegar, salt and pepper, and whisk until slightly thickened. Arrange the lettuce leaves on individual serving plates. Spoon the dressing over just before serving and sprinkle with the chives.

Nan Paul   *Grant School, Escondido*

Sumi Salad

Yields 10 (½ cup) servings

2 tablespoons oil
¼ cup almonds, sliced
¼ cup sesame seeds
8 green onions, finely sliced

1 head cabbage, finely chopped
2 3 oz. packages Ramen noodles
    broken (reserve seasoning packet
    for another use.)
Dressing

Heat oil in skillet and toast almonds and seeds until lightly browned. Combine with onions, cabbage, noodles and dressing. Cover and chill several hours for flavors to blend.

Dressing:

¼ cup sugar
1 teaspoon black pepper
1 teaspoon salt

1 cup oil
6 tablespoons rice vinegar
2 teaspoons MSG, optional

Combine sugar, pepper, salt, oil, vinegar and MSG. Mix well.

This recipe was selected as one of the top 10 recipes published in 1983 by the Los Angeles Times staff.

Maggie Aguirre   *Auburndale Junior High School, Corona*

Antipasto Salad

Celery
Cauliflower
Carrots
Mushrooms
Green Pepper

1 can black pitted olives
1 jar whole artichoke hearts
½ red onion rings, sliced
½ cup sweet Italian wax peppers
Pepperoni or salami, sliced

Wash and cut the vegetables into bite size pieces. Blanch vegetables one at a time in a covered dish with no water added by cooking as follows: (Cooking time is for 1 cup of vegetables) Celery: cut diagonally, cook 45 seconds to 1 minute. Cauliflower: cut into flowers, cook 2 minutes. Carrots: cut diagonally, cook 1 to 1½ minutes. Mushrooms: whole button size, cook 30 to 45 seconds. Green pepper: cut in strips, cook 25 to 30 seconds. After blanching each vegetable, put into a plastic strainer and place in ice water to stop the cooking. Drain all vegetables well before adding marinade. Add the remaining ingredients to the blanched vegetables and toss in a large bowl with marinade (see recipe below).

Marinade:

⅓ cup tarragon wine vinegar
½ teaspoon salt
1 teaspoon basil

⅔ cup salad oil
2 cloves garlic, pressed or minced
½ teaspoon pepper

Whisk above ingredients together in food processor or blender. Pour over blanched vegetables. Serve chilled. Best to marinate overnight.

Marilyn Pereira   *Hanford Union High School, Hanford*

Tuna Vegetable Salad

Serves 4

1 6½ oz. can chunk white tuna,
  drained
1 cup celery, sliced
1 cup carrots, grated
1 medium onion, finely minced

3 tablespoons mayonnaise
2 tablespoons pickle relish
1 #2½ size can shoestring
  potatoes
salt and pepper to taste

In mixing bowl, toss tuna, celery, and carrots; set aside. Combine onion, mayonnaise and relish thoroughly in small bowl. Toss with tuna mixture. Add shoestring potatoes just before serving. Season to taste. Serve on a bed of lettuce, if desired.

I serve this with quartered fresh tomatoes arranged around the salad. It makes a very quick, satisfying meal during the hot summer months.

Clyle Alt   *Bell Gardens High School, Bell Gardens*

Salad Supreme

1 cup carrots, grated or shredded
   (wash, peel and cut off ends)
1/2 cup celery, diced
1 tablespoon onion, grated or diced

1 can tuna, drained
1 cup mayonnaise
1 can shoestring potatoes

Combine all ingredients except the shoestring potatoes which are added just before serving, so that they will remain crisp.

Marianne Traw   *Ball Junior High School, Anaheim*

Shrimp Salad

Serves 4

1 6 oz. can shrimp
1 cup celery, chopped
1 cup lettuce, chopped
1 cup carrot, grated

1 teaspon onion, minced
1 can dried chinese noodles
1/4 cup mayonnaise

Drain shrimp, reserving liquid. Prepare and mix salad ingredients and add shrimp. Just before serving add noodles. Mix mayonnaise with some shrimp juice to thin and toss.

Loretta Salau   *Foothill High School, Bakersfield*

Make-ahead Chutney Chicken Salad

Yields 5 cups

2 tablespoons Major Grey's chutney
1/2 teaspoon curry
1/2 cup mayonnaise
1/2 cup sour cream or yogurt

2 1/2 cups chicken
   cooked and cubed
1/2 cup water chestnuts, sliced
1 cup pineapple tidbits
1/2 cup celery, sliced

Combine first 4 ingredients to make salad dressing. Toss with other ingredients. Refrigerate for 24 hours. Serve chilled on lettuce leaf.

Cook chicken ahead or use leftovers for this tasty recipe.

Joan Irvine   *Upland High School, Upland*

Teriyaki Chicken Salad

Serves 2

2 teaspoons dry sherry
1 tablespoon soy sauce
1 tablespoon brown sugar
1/8 teaspoon fresh ginger, grated
1 small clove garlic, minced
3 tablespoons peanut oil

1 5 oz. can white chicken, drained
1/2 red bell pepper, cut in thin
strips 1 1/2 inches long
1/2 cup snow peas,
cut in half diagonally
1/2 cup Chinese cabbage,
thinly sliced

In medium bowl, mix first six ingredients; stir until sugar dissolves and mixture is well blended. Add remaining ingredients and toss gently to mix.

This is good served with crunchy fried won ton wrappers.

Carole Delap   *Golden West High School, Visalia*

Family Taco Salad

Serves 4 to 6

1 lb. ground beef
1 onion, chopped
seasonings to taste
½ head lettuce, shredded
1 cup cheese, grated
   (cheddar or jack)

1 can black olives, sliced
1 can kidney beans, drained
1 can ortega chiles, diced
2 tomatoes, chopped
1 bag taco chips or fritos, or
   tortilla chips
taco sauce

Brown ground beef and onion in skillet. Drain off fat. Add seasonings to taste, (salt, pepper, chili powder, taco seasoning mix or etc.). Place meat mixture in a large bowl and add remaining ingredients.

Serve with guacamole, garnish and fresh fruit dessert. Add or take away ingredients to suit family taste.

Sally Oxford   **Monache High School, Porterville**

Taco Salad

Serves 6 to 8

1 lb. hamburger
1 package taco seasoning mix
4 to 6 oz. cheddar cheese
2 to 3 tomatoes, sliced
1 head iceberg lettuce

Brown hamburger and add taco mix. Prepare, following taco seasoning mix directions. Shred lettuce and grate the cheese. Put seasoned hamburger over the lettuce and add the cheese and sliced tomatoes.

Faye Nielsen   **Rosemead High School, Rosemead**

Festive Frozen Salad

Serves 12

1 cup sour cream
1 tablespoon lemon juice
¼ cup sugar
1/8 teaspoon salt
1 8 oz. can crushed pineapple,
   drained

1 banana, diced
4 drops food coloring
½ cup nuts, chopped
1 1 lb. can pitted bing cherries,
   well drained

Combine sour cream, lemon juice, sugar, salt, drained crushed pineapple, diced banana and food coloring. Lightly fold in nuts and drained cherries. Spoon into paper muffin cups that have been placed into muffin tins. Freeze. (Once frozen, muffin tins can be removed and frozen salads placed in large plastic bag and returned to freezer.) When ready to use peel off paper muffin cups 15 minutes before serving and place on a lettuce bed.

Beverly McNulty   **Lindhurst High School, Olivehurst**

Soups, Sandwiches
&
Crock Pot Cookery

Seven Minute Clam Chowder

Serves 4

1 cup potatoes, cubed
¼ teaspoon salt
¼ cup margarine
1 slice bacon, finely chopped
3 tablespoons flour
¼ cup onions, chopped

1 7¼ oz. can minced clams,
  undrained
1 cup light cream
¼ teaspoon pepper
¼ teaspoon dried parsley
½ cup milk

Peel and cut potatoes into 1/4 to 3/8 inch cubes. Place in small saucepan, barely cover with water; add ¼ teaspoon salt. Cover and bring to a boil, reduce heat and continue cooking until they are just fork tender, drain. In a 1½ quart glass baking dish, combine butter, finely chopped bacon, flour and chopped onion. Cook in microwave oven for 2 minutes. Stir in remaining ingredients. Cook for 3 minutes, stir; cook 2 minutes longer or until thickened. Add drained potatoes and cook until heated through. Allow to stand several minutes before serving.

More clams may be added, according to taste.

Eleanor Magorien   **El Toro High School, El Toro**

Gold Coast Fish Chowder

Serves 4

1 cup onion, chopped
½ cup celery, chopped
1 clove garlic, crushed
2 tablespoons butter
2 16 oz. cans tomatoes
½ cup dry white wine

½ cup parsley, minced
1 teaspoon salt
¼ teaspoon thyme
¼ teaspoon pepper
1 lb. frozen fish fillets
1 lb. cocktail shrimp

In a large pot, saute onion, celery and garlic in butter. Stir in tomatoes, wine, parsley, salt, pepper and thyme. Cover and simmer 20 minutes. While tomato mixture is simmering, cut fillets into chunks. Add fish and shrimp. Simmer an additional 7 to 10 minutes.

Serve with crusty French bread.

Nanci Burkhart   **Hueneme High School, Oxnard**

Greek Lemon Soup

Serves 8

¼ lb. butter
2 quarts chicken stock with
  chicken pieces
1 teaspoon powdered chicken stock

½ cup sauterne
3 egg yolks
juice of 2 lemons
parsley

Simmer butter, stock, powdered stock and wine for 20 minutes. In a separate bowl, beat yolks and lemon until frothy (may use blender for this step). Whisk 1 cup hot soup into egg yolks and add all to soup. Garnish with parsley.

Judy Hevener   **Porterville High School, Porterville**

Kielbasa Soup

Serves 4

1 medium potato, peeled and diced
2 carrots, sliced
2 medium onion, chopped

1/3 cup celery, chopped
3 cups boiling water
8 oz. Kielbasa sausage, thinly sliced
1 10 1/2 oz. can bean 'n bacon soup

Add diced potatoes, sliced carrots, and chopped onion and celery to boiling water. Cover and cook for about 10 minutes or until vegetables are tender. Add Kielbasa sausage and bean soup and heat thoroughly.

This is a wonderful quick and hearty soup for a chilly day.

Harriet Trousdale   **Roosevelt Junior High School, Glendale**

Quick Vegetable Soup

Makes about 4 cups

1/4 cup onion, diced
1/4 cup carrot, diced
1/4 cup celery, diced
2 tablespoons butter
1 1/2 cup beef or chicken broth
1 cup canned tomatoes with juices, chopped
1/2 cup potatoes, diced

1/2 cup other vegetables (peas, corn, zucchini, green beans, beets, cabbage, etc.)
1 tablespoon parsley, minced
1/2 teaspoon basil leaves, crumbled
1/2 teaspoon marjoram or oregano leaves crumbled
1/2 teaspoon salt
1/8 teaspoon pepper

In large saucepan, saute onion, carrot, and celery in butter until onions are transparent. Add broth, tomatoes, potatoes, other vegetables, parsley. Cover and cook for 35 minutes until vegetables are tender.

1/2 cup pasta (macaroni, noodles, spaghetti) may be added the last 15 minutes of the cooking period, if desired.

Dot Rhodes   **Upland High School, Upland**

Meatball Soup

Serves 6 to 8

1 large 28 oz. can tomatoes
3 cups water
1 bay leaf
1 lb. ground round

1/2 cup Minute rice
salt to taste
pepper to taste
1/2 package Chili Seasoning Mix

Heat tomatoes and water in 2 quart sauce pan until boiling. Add bay leaf and simmer 6 minutes. Mix ground round, rice and salt and pepper. Shape into 1 inch balls. Add chili seasoning mix to tomatoes. Drop meatballs gently into tomaotes. Cover and simmer for 20 minutes.

Good served with garlic bread.

Bonnie Parks   **Big Pine High School, Big Pine**

Creamy Farmer's Soup

Serves 4

1 cup water
1 chicken bouillon cube
1/2 cup potatoes, diced
1/4 cup carrots, sliced
2 tablespoons green pepper,
   chopped

1/4 cup onion, chopped
1 tablespoon margarine
dash of salt
3 tablespoons flour
1 1/2 cups whole milk
1 cup cheddar cheese, grated

Boil 1 cup water in medium sauce pan. Add bouillon cube. Stir until dissolved. Add vegetables, margarine and salt. Bring to a boil. Reduce heat and simmer until vegetables are fork tender, about 10 minutes. Mix flour and milk until smooth. Add flour, milk mixture to vegetables and cook for 3 minutes to thicken. Stir in cheese. Heat until well blended and smooth.

Jeannie Burns   *Los Osos Junior High School, Los Osos*

Bean Chalupa

Serves 6 to 8

1 lb. pinto beans
3 lbs. pork roast
7 cups water
1/2 cup onion, chopped
2 cloves garlic

1 tablespoon salt
2 tablespoons chili powder
1 tablespoon cumin
1 teaspoon oregano
1 4 oz. can chopped chilies

Put ingredients into large crock pot in order listed after dinner. Cook all night and the following day on low. Serve that night with tortillas or over rice. Use a little less water if making into burritos. Toppings such as tomatoes, avocado, cheese and sour cream are especially good when using as burritos.

Can be frozen for later use after cooking. Great for company.

Kim Frost   *Tulare Union High School, Tulare*

Gazpacho

Yields approximately 2 quarts

2 cans baby tomatoes, sliced and
   chopped finely (including juice,
   approximately 3 cups)
1/2 cup cucumber, finely chopped
1/2 cup green pepper, finely chopped
1/2 cup green onion, finely chopped
1/2 cup celery, finely chopped

2 cloves garlic, minced
1 tablespoon olive oil or
   vegetable oil
3 tablespoons wine vinegar
1 teaspoon worcestershire sauce
1 12 oz. can V-8 juice
1 can condensed beef broth
liquid hot pepper sauce, to taste

Combine all ingredients and chill thoroughly. Serve in chilled glass cups or champagne glasses. May be garnished with cucumber slices, chopped green onion, or croutons. Makes about two quarts.

Dot Rhodes   *Upland High School, Upland*

Cucumber Soup

Serves 2

1 cucumber, peeled	½ teaspoon salt
1 small section garlic clove, cut	parsley, chopped
1 cup chicken broth	green onions, chopped
1 cup sour cream	tomatoes, chopped
1 tablespoon vinegar	salted and blanched almonds, chopped

Whirl cucumbers and garlic with a little of the broth in blender until smooth. Blend with remaining broth. Stir a little of this mixture into sour cream, then stir into cucumber liquid. Season with vinegar and salt. Cover and chill. Serve in bowls with parsley, green onion, tomatoes and salted blanched almonds to spoon over top.

Lorraine Pepper   *Oceanside High School, Oceanside*

Crab Bisque

Serves 6 to 8

1 can mushroom soup	1 soup can milk
1 can asparagus soup	1 ¼ cup cream or half and half
¾ lb. crab	¼ cup sherry
	Butter

Blend soup, crab, milk and cream. Add sherry at the last minute. Float a slice of butter on the top of each serving.

Judy Hevener   *Porterville High School, Porterville*

Boston Clam Chowder

Serves 4 to 6

7 oz. can clams, minced	2 potatoes, peeled and thinly sliced
4 slices bacon, chopped	½ teaspoon salt
¼ cup chopped onions (more if desired)	¼ teaspoon pepper
liquid drained from clams plus water to make 1 cup	2½ cups milk
	2 tablespoons butter
	parsley for garnish (optional)

Drain clams and save liquid. Fry bacon and onions until bacon is lightly browned and onions are tender and transparent. Add liquid (from clams plus water), potatoes and seasonings. Cook, covered over medium heat for 15 minutes or until potatoes are tender. Add milk, clams and butter. Heat but do not boil. Serve piping hot, with parsley on top.

A food processor really speeds this up. It's good served with a hot bread and green salad.

Polly Frank   *Lakewood High School, Lakewood*

Grandma Charles' Tomato Bisque Soup

Serves 6

½ onion, chopped
2 stalks celery, chopped
½ cup butter
¼ cup flour
1 quart milk

1½ teaspoons salt
1 teaspoon parsley, chopped
1 quart stewed tomatoes
¼ teaspoon soda

Saute onions and celery in butter for 5 minutes; then add flour and cook 1 minute. Stir in milk, salt and parsley; cook in double boiler for 20 minutes. Cook tomatoes in separate pan and press through sieve (if desired). Add soda to tomatoes just before combining the two mixtures. Slowly add the hot tomato mixture to milk mixture and serve immediately.

Becca Charles   *Amador County High School, Sutter Creek*

Auntie Jean's Crab Sandwiches

Serves 8 (or 16 slices)

1 loaf french bread
2 cans crab meat, drained
butter

garlic
mayonnaise
Cheez Whiz

Slice the loaf of French bread lengthwise. Drain 2 cans of crab meat and mix with enough mayonnaise to spread easily. Mix softened butter with garlic to suit your individual taste. Butter both bread halves with garlic butter. Spread a generous covering of Cheez Whiz on top of garlic butter. Spread the crab and mayonnaise mixture over the Cheez Whiz. Wrap each half loaf separately in tin foil. This delicious sandwich can be made ahead of time and stored in refrigerator before heating and serving. When ready to serve, place in 350° oven and bake for 20 minutes. Slice, serve and enjoy.

I use this recipe as a snack or appetizer.

Gerry Wuesthoff   **Lexington Junior High School, Cypress**

Valencia Sandwiches

Serves 1

1 slice of bread
1 slice of avocado or tomato

1 slice of American cheese
1 slice of bacon or ham
mayonnaise or butter if desired

Toast slice of bread in broiler. Watch carefully not to burn. Butter or spread with mayonnaise. Place 1 slice avocado or slice of tomato on toast. Cover with a slice of cheese over bacon or ham. Place the open face sandwich in broiler just until cheese has melted.

Lou Helen Yergat   **Mission Viejo High School, Mission Viejo**

Corned Beef Sandwiches

Serves 6

1 can corned beef
2 cups cheddar cheese, grated
1 small can olives, sliced

½ onion, finely chopped (optional)
1 cup catsup
butter
1 package sour dough rolls

Flake corned beef into a mixing bowl. Add cheese, olives, and onion; mix well. Add catsup and mix to moisten. You may need to add more catsup to develop spreading consistency. Slice rolls and butter each half. Mound on corned beef mixture and top with sliced roll. Wrap sandwiches in foil and bake at 350° for about 30 minutes or until cheese melts and mixture becomes hot.

This recipe was given to me many years ago by Mrs. Joan Frost and used for several skiing trips. You may prepare these sandwiches ahead of time and store them in the refrigerator before baking, or you may bake and wrap them in a towel and keep warm until ready to serve.

donor not named

Chicken Salad Burrito

Serves 6

6 tablespoons sour cream
¼ cup hot taco sauce
1 teaspoon cumin
¾ teaspoon chili powder
1 5 oz. can chunk white chicken,
   drained

½ cup avocado, chopped
½ cup tomatoes, chopped
2 tablespoon diced Ortega chiles
¼ cup lettuce, shredded
6 flour tortillas

In medium bowl, combine first four ingredients. Add chicken, avocado, tomato and chiles and gently toss to mix. Place ¼ cup of salad mixture and some lettuce on each flour tortilla; fold bottom up and over salad mixture. Fold sides in and roll up until salad mixture is enclosed completely. Wrap each tortilla in clear plastic wrap to hold shape and keep fresh until ready to serve.

Great for a faculty luncheon!

Carole Delap   **Golden West High School, Visalia**

Steak Burritos

Tender steak
seasoned salt and pepper
large flour tortillas
ortega whole chiles, cut lengthwise

jack cheese, grated
cheddar cheese, grated
salsa, mild to hot (bottled)
avocado, sliced (optional)

Broil or barbecue steak seasoned with seasoned salt and pepper. Medium rare makes these burritos especially delicious. Slice steak into thin strips. Warm tortillas on ungreased skillet until pliable. Place a few steak strips, chili strips, grated cheese and 1 tablespoon of salsa on each tortilla. Fold tortilla around the mixture burrito style, leaving one end open. Heat on ungreased skillet until cheese melts. Remove from heat and if desired slip avocado slice into open end of burrito.

Serving suggestion: Prepare instant Spanish rice and canned spicy refried beans as accompaniments along with tortilla chips.

I like to prepare the ingredients and allow family or guests to assemble their own burritos and serve buffet style.

Sharon Turner   **El Dorado High School, Placentia**

Cheese 'n Wiener Crescents

Hot dogs
Sharp cheddar cheese
Pillsbury crescent rolls

Slit hot dogs to within ½ inch of ends; insert strips of sharp cheddar cheese; place hot dog on shortest side of Pillsbury Crescent dough triangle; roll up; place cheese side up on cookie sheet. Bake at 375° for 12 to 15 minutes or until golden brown.

Lynn Robertson   **Esparto High School, Esparto**

Sloppy Joe's

Serves 4

1 lb. ground beef
1/2 teaspoon salt
2 tablespoon molasses
2 tablespoons prepared mustard

1 tablespoon worcestershire sauce
1/8 teaspoon hot pepper sauce
1/2 cup catsup
4 hamburger buns or
   sourdough bread

Brown beef and drain any grease. Add remaining ingredients and heat until well blended. Serve on hamburger buns or sourdough bread. Chopped onion and/or celery can be cooked with the hamburger if desired.

Fast and easy!

Nancy Byrum   **Patrick Henry High School, San Diego**

Open Face Toasted Cheese Sandwiches

Serves 1 to 2

1/2 cup grated parmesan cheese
1/2 cup sharp cheddar cheese
1/4 cup mayonnaise
1/4 cup plain yogurt

1/4 cup sunflower seeds
1/4 cup onion, chopped
1/4 cup parsley, chopped
dash of garlic powder

Combine all ingredients well and spread on your favorite bread or english muffin. Broil until brown and puffy. Garnish with slice of olive and paprika.

A quick and easy lunch when combined with a leafy green salad!

Julie Sherrill   **Dos Palos High School, Dos Palos**

Pizza Fiestas Ⓜ

Serves 4 to 6

4 7 inch flour tortillas
16 oz. can refried beans
1/2 cup green onion, sliced
1/2 cup green pepper, sliced

1/4 cup ripe olives, sliced
1/2 cup tomato, cubed (if desired)
1/2 teaspoon chili powder
8 oz. Colby cheese, shredded

Heat oven to 350°. Bake tortillas on ungreased cookie sheet for 5 minutes. Cool. Gently spread each tortilla with 1/3 cup refried beans. On each tortilla layer 2 tablespoons green onion, 2 tablespoons green pepper, 1 tablespoon olives and 2 tablespoons tomato. Sprinkle with 1/8 teaspoon chili powder and 1/2 cup cheese. Bake 8 to 10 minutes or until cheese melts or microwave 1 minute each. Cut into wedges. Serve warm. Yield: 4 individual pizzas.

This recipe can be totally vegetarian with the use of 'vegetarian refried beans and vegetarian flour tortillas'. These appetizers can be made ahead and microwaved at the last moment before serving, 30 to 45 seconds on high.

Shirley Blough   **Hillside Junior High School, Simi Valley**

Tostadas

Serves 4

4 stone ground corn tortillas
oil for frying
½ can refried beans, heated
    according to package directions
1 cup lettuce, shredded
1 tomato, sliced
½ avocado, peeled, seeded
    and sliced

Monterey jack or
    Mozzarella cheese, shredded
½ cup dairy sour cream
4 ripe olives, sliced or
    1 tablespoons chopped olives
Hot beef filling

Fry tortillas on both sides in small amount of oil until crisp. Drain on paper towels. Spread each tortilla with refried beans and then with Hot Beef filling. Top with shredded lettuce, tomato slice, and avocado slices. Sprinkle with cheese. Garnish with sour cream and ripe olives.

Hot Beef Filling

½ small onion, minced
½ clove garlic, minced
1 tablespoon cooking oil
½ pound ground beef

2 tablespoons ripe olives, chopped
½ envelope taco seasoning mix
salt
pepper

Cook onion and garlic in oil for 3 minutes. Add meat and brown. Add olives and taco seasoning mix. Simmer until heated through. Season with salt and pepper to taste.

Lou Yergat   Mission Viejo High School, Mission Viejo

Sausage Appetizers Ⓜ

2 to 3 lbs. sweet sausage, mini links
1 8 oz. bottle Chris 'N Pits BBQ Sauce
½ package brown sugar
1 tablespoon dry mustard

Put all ingredients in crock pot for 4 to 6 hours or simmer in microwave for 20 minutes or simmer on stove for approximately 45 minutes to 1 hour. Serve with toothpicks.

Wanda Baral   **Crest View School, Huntington Beach**

Chili-Cheese Dip

Serves 10 to 12

1 lb. ground beef   *2 teaspoons worcestershire sauce*
2 lbs. Velveeta cheese   *½ teaspoon chili powder*
1 8 to 10 oz. can chili salsa

Brown ground beef. Drain grease. Using a crock pot, slowly melt cheese. Add beef and remaining ingredients. Keep warm in crock pot. Serve with chips.

NOTE: You may want to add less salsa for a milder flavor.

A student made this for the class and it was a big hit!

Cathy Smith   **Lone Hill Intermediate School, San Dimas**

Dotti's Mexican Beans

Serves 10 to 12

4 cups pinto beans   *2 teaspoons salt or to taste*
1 large onion   *1 teaspoon garlic powder*
2 large tomatoes or 1 can of   *1 teaspoon cumin seeds*
*   stewed tomatoes*   *1 teaspoon ground pepper*
8 oz. salt pork or ham hock   *1 jalapeno pepper*

Soak beans in water overnight. Rinse. Place beans in crock pot, cover with water. Add all the ingredients listed above. Cook on high for 10 to 12 hours. Check water level occasionally.

Can be served with cornbread or mashed and used as refrieds. Good for company meal. May be frozen easily.

Dotti Jones   **Etiwanda High School, Etiwanda**

No Peek

Serves 8

2 pounds cubed beef   *1 package dried onion soup*
2 cans Golden Mushroom Soup,   *1 8 oz. can mushrooms*
*   undiluted*   *½ cup red wine vinegar*

Mix all ingredients. Place in a 2 quart casserole dish; cover and bake at 300° for 3 hours. Serve with noodles or rice. Crock pot method: Low temperature 8 to 12 hours or high 5 to 6 hours.

Roberta S. Priestley   **Alhambra High School, Alhambra**

Breads

Herbed Bread

½ lb. butter or margarine, softened
1 teaspoon parsley flakes
1 teaspoon dill weed

¼ teaspoon oregano flakes
garlic to taste
1 loaf French bread, sliced

Soften butter and combine with other ingredients. Spread on bread slices and put loaf back together. Wrap in foil but leave top open. Sprinkle with parmesan cheese. Bake at 400°F for 15 to 20 minutes.

I always get compliments on this product when I serve it, and I have passed on this recipe to many friends and family members.

Doris L. Oitzman   **Victor Valley High School, Victorville**

Shirley's Pizza Crust

1 tablespoon dry yeast
1 cup lukewarm water
2 teaspoons sugar

1½ teaspoons salt
1 tablespoon shortening
1 egg, beaten
3 to 4 cups flour

Dissolve yeast in warm water. Add sugar, salt, and shortening and egg. Stir in flour until dough sticks together. Knead lightly until dough can be rolled out. Place on lightly greased cookie sheet. Top with your favorite stuff!

A very fast and tasty pizza crust.

Leonda Lines   **Leuzinger High School, Lawndale**

Quick Garlic Sticks

Yields 20 sticks

2 cups rice, wheat or corn chex
1 teaspoon garlic powder
¼ teaspoon salt

4 tablespoons margarine, melted
1 package refrigerated biscuits

Heat oven to 450°. Crush chex and combine with garlic powder and salt. Add 2 tablespoons margarine. Mix well. Cut each biscuit in half. Roll between palms of hands into sticks 8 inches long. Brush with remaining melted margarine. Coat with crumbs. Bake on ungreased baking sheet 7 minutes or until golden brown.

Madelyn V. Fielding   **Jordan High School, Long Beach**

Buttermilk Pancakes or Waffles

Yields about 18 pancakes or 8 waffles

2 cups white flour
1¾ cups whole wheat flour
1 tablespoon baking powder
1 teaspoon baking soda

1 teaspoon salt
2 tablespoons sugar
2 cups buttermilk
3 tablespoons oil
2 eggs, separated

Carefully measure the first six ingredients into a medium sized bowl. Add buttermilk, oil, and egg yolks to dry ingredients and stir until blended. Beat egg whites until stiff and fold into pancake batter very carefully.

Donna Swennes   **El Capitan High School, Lakeside**

Bread Sticks

Yields 32 bread sticks

4 tablespoons butter or margarine	1 tablespoon sugar
2 cups biscuit mix	½ cup milk

Melt butter in 13x9 inch pan in oven. Combine biscuit mix, sugar and milk in mixing bowl. Stir with a fork until a soft dough is formed. Beat vigorously 20 strokes until stiff but still sticky. Turn out on board lightly dusted with biscuit mix. Knead gently about 10 times. Roll to a 12x8 inch rectangle. With floured knife, cut dough in half lengthwise. Cut each half crosswise into 16 strips. Dip each strip in melted butter in pan, turning to coat both sides. Arrange strips in 2 rows. Bake about 12 minutes in 400° oven until golden brown. Serve warm.

Variation: ½ cup grated cheese may be added to dough before cutting, or sesame seeds may be sprinkled on top after butter before baking.

Jill S. Anderson   *Santa Paula Union High School, Santa Paula*

Cold Oven Pecan Rolls

Serves 12

24 frozen dinner rolls	¾ cup brown sugar
1 package butterscotch pudding	chopped pecans or
mix (not instant)	slivered almonds
4 tablespoons butter	dash of cinnamon

Grease a 9x13 inch pan. Arrange frozen rolls in pan. Sprinkle butterscotch pudding over the top of frozen rolls. Distribute small pieces of butter on and around frozen rolls. Sprinkle brown sugar over rolls. Distribute chopped nuts evenly over rolls. Shake cinnamon lightly over rolls. Put pan of rolls in **cold** oven. (Gas pilot can cause these to rise too much, so put pan in oven just before you go to bed.) In the morning **do not open oven door!** Turn oven to 350° and bake 20 to 25 minutes or until golden brown. Turn onto plate while rolls are hot.

These can be prepared ahead of time. Cover with foil and keep ready to put in oven when needed.

Pat Fiscus   *Sinaloa Junior High School, Simi Valley*

Corn Bread

Serves 9 to 12

2 cups Bisquick	2 eggs
½ cup cornmeal	1 cup milk
¾ to 1 cup sugar	½ cup margarine, melted

Combine bisquick mix, cornmeal and sugar in mixer bowl. Add eggs and milk. Beat until well blended. Mix in melted butter. Place in greased 9 inch square pan. Bake 350° for 30 to 40 minutes or when golden brown and toothpick comes out clean.

Julie Hampton   *Franklin Junior High School, Long Beach*

Butterscotch Rolls

Serves 8

25 oz. frozen dinner rolls
3½ oz. butterscotch pudding
(not instant)
1 cup brown sugar

¼ cup sugar
1 teaspoon cinnamon
½ cup pecans, chopped
½ cup butter, melted

Place frozen rolls in greased bundt pan. Mix butterscotch pudding and brown sugar; sprinkle over frozen rolls. Combine sugar and cinnamon and sprinkle over the last mixture. Place chopped pecans on top, pour melted butter over pecans. Let set overnight or at least eight hours, then bake at 350° for 30 minutes.

This recipe is neat because you prepare it the night before, then cook in the morning and it makes your house smell terrific. It stays moist and sticky. Excellent with coffee!

Marsha R. Martin **Auburndale Junior High School, Corona**

All Bran Molasses Muffins (no fat)

Yields 12

2 cups bran cereal
½ cup molasses
1½ cups milk
1 egg

1 cup whole wheat flour
½ teaspoon salt
1 teaspoon soda

Add cereal to molasses, add milk and allow to soak for 15 minutes. Beat egg and add to first mixture. Stir in flour, salt, and soda and mix lightly. Fill greased muffin pans ⅔ full and bake at 400° for 20 minutes.

Donna Swennes **El Capitan High School, Lakeside**

Orange Bread

Yields 30 muffins or 2 loaves

1 Valencia orange
3 eggs
2 cups sugar
1 cup oil
3 cups flour, unsifted
½ teaspoon salt

½ teaspoon baking powder
1 teaspoon baking soda
¼ teaspoon cinnamon
1 small can crushed pineapple,
drained
½ cup chopped walnuts

Quarter a Valencia orange, remove seeds. Put it through a blender or processor until very finely chopped (nearly pureed). Don't remove peel, "trust me!" Beat eggs until frothy; add sugar, orange and oil. Add all dry ingredients and mix well. Stir in pineapple and nuts. Pour into muffin tins or 2 large loaf pans. Bake at 325° for 30 minutes or 1 hour for loaf.

Grinding up an unpeeled orange sounds disgusting, but the muffins are delicious and healthy!

Ginny Loranger **Luther Burbank Junior High School, Burbank**

Breakfast Cookies

Yields 2 dozen

1 cup flour (unsifted)
¾ cup sugar
¼ teaspoon baking soda

½ lb. cooked crisp bacon
1 egg
2 cups flake cereal (corn flakes)

Mix flour, sugar and baking soda in a bowl. Stir in cooked bacon and egg. Add cornflakes. Drop by tablespoons onto ungreased cookie sheet. Bake 350° for 13 to 15 minutes. Let stand before removing.

You may also divide the dough in half and form 2 inch diameter rolls; wrap in wax paper and freeze. Slice ¼ inch thick and bake at 400° for 8 to 10 minutes.

Ham may be substituted for bacon; use ½ cup small cubes or thin sliced, like Julienne.

Who says there's no time to eat breakfast? These are great for a change. Bake some; freeze some for tomorrow.

Sharletta Kay Myers   **DeMille Junior High School, Long Beach**

Ham and Cheese Crescent Buns

Serves 8

3 oz. package thinly sliced ham
½ cup cheddar cheese, shredded
2 tablespoons onion, finely chopped

½ teaspoon garlic salt
8 oz. can crescent rolls
2 teaspoons margarine

Preheat oven to 375°. Grease 8 muffin cups. In a small bowl, combine first 4 ingredients. Separate crescent dough into 8 triangles. Spoon meat mixture on wide end of each triangle. Top with ¼ teaspoon margarine. Wrap dough around mixture and press edges of dough tightly to seal. Place in greased muffin tins. Bake at 375° for 20 to 25 minutes or until golden brown.

Judy Hevener   **Porterville High School, Porterville**

Orange Nut Bread

Serves 8 to 10

1 orange, chopped
boiling hot water
1 teaspoon baking soda
1 cup sugar
1 tablespoon butter, melted
1 teaspoon vanilla

1 egg, beaten
1 cup flour
¼ teaspoon salt
1 teaspoon baking powder
½ cup walnuts

Preheat oven to 350°. Squeeze juice from orange and add boiling water to orange juice to equal 1 cup. Chop up orange and add to liquid. Stir in baking soda, sugar, melted butter, vanilla and egg. Sift flour, salt, and baking powder. Mix all ingredients until blended. Stir in chopped nuts. Bake 45 to 50 minutes.

This recipe takes approximately 50 minutes to bake, but it's very easy and quick to prepare!

Linda Leo   **La Sierra High School, Riverside**

Almond Poppy Seed Bread

Yields 2 loaves

3 cups flour
2¾ cups sugar
1½ cups baking powder
1½ teaspoons salt
3 eggs
1½ cups milk
1½ cups oil
2 tablespoons poppy seeds
1 tablespoon vanilla extract

1 tablespoon almond extract
1 tablespoon butternut extract

Glaze
¼ cup orange juice
¾ cup sugar
½ teaspoon vanilla extract
½ teaspoon almond extract
½ teaspoon butternut extract

Sift together dry ingredients and set aside. Mix together eggs, milk and oil. Add to dry ingredients. Add poppy seeds and flavorings. Beat together two minutes. Bake in 2 greased and floured loaf pans at 350° for 45 to 60 minutes.

Glaze: Place all ingredients in a saucepan. Bring to a boil, stirring constantly. Let simmer five minutes. Brush on warm bread.

Delicious! Great for gifts during the holidays.

Bonnie Landin   *Garden Grove High School, Garden Grove*

Port Wine Jelly

Yields 4 to 8 jars

3 cups sugar
2 cups port wine
½ bottle liquid pectin

Prepare four 8 oz. canning jars and lids. In top of double boiler stir sugar and wine together. Heat until sugar dissolves (about 5 minutes). Remove from heat. Stir in pectin. Pour into jars and seals.

I use this with cheddar cheese and crackers and for gift giving. This jelly is such a pretty color! I usually put a jar in a basket along with a couple of kinds of cheese and crackers and give it as a small gift at Christmas or Valentine's Day."

Gwenn Jensen   *Mira Mesa High School, San Diego*

Speedy Cinnamon Ring

Serves 4

1 package refrigerator biscuits
2 tablespoons butter or margarine, melted
¼ cup brown sugar
1 teaspoon cinnamon

Dip biscuits in melted butter or margarine then in cinnamon sugar mixture. Place in cake or pie pan in ring shape, overlapping a little bit. Bake at 425° for 13 to 15 minutes.

Leona Rice   *Awahnee Middle School, Fresno*

Parsley Refrigerator Rolls

2 tablespoons butter or margarine
parsley, dried and crushed
1 package refrigerator rolls

Melt butter in cake pan and crush parsley into butter. Add rolls. Bake according to directions on container. Remove and serve hot.

Donna Kinney   *Laguna Junior High School, San Luis Obispo*

Double "B" Muffins

Yield 10

1 cup all purpose flour
3 tablespoons sugar
2½ teaspoons baking powder
½ teaspoon salt
1 cup whole bran

1 egg, well beaten
1 cup ripe bananas, mashed
½ cup milk
2 tablespoons salad oil

Turn oven to 400° to preheat. Sift together flour, sugar, baking powder, salt. Stir in bran. Mix remaining ingredients; add all at once to the flour mixture. Stir mixture just enough to moisten. Grease 10 muffin tins; fill ⅔ full. Bake 20 to 25 minutes.

Delicious breakfast treat with fresh fruit.

Cheryl A. Oravetz   *Hemet High School, Hemet*

Sunshine Rolls

Yields 8 rolls

¼ cup sugar
1 tablespoon grated orange rind
  (orange color only)
1 can Pillsbury crescent
  dinner rolls
1 tablespoon melted butter

Glaze:

¼ cup sugar
¼ cup sour cream
1 tablespoon orange juice
3 tablespoons butter

Preheat oven to 350°. Combine ¼ cup sugar and 1 tablespoon orange rind. Remove crescent dinner rolls from can and lay dough flat on working surface without separating individual pieces of dough. Brush generously with melted butter. Spoon sugar mixture over dough spreading evenly. Roll up crescents breaking perforations as you go. Place point side down in 8x8 inch baking dish or pan. Bake at 350° for about 15 minutes or until golden. Top with glaze.

Glaze: Combine ingredients and boil for 3 minutes stirring constantly. Pour over rolls when removed from oven.

Dot Rhodes   *Upland High School, Upland*

Recipe for "Fruit Tart" on page 118 ➡

Date Nut Muffins

Yields 12 muffins

1 package (8 oz.) pitted dates,
  coarsely chopped
¾ cup boiling water
¼ cup Mazola corn oil
½ teaspoon vanilla

1 cup unsifted flour
½ cup unsifted whole wheat flour
½ cup sugar
⅓ cup coarsely chopped walnuts
½ teaspoon baking soda

Grease 12 2½x1¼ inch muffin cups. In medium bowl stir together dates, boiling water, corn oil and vanilla. In small bowl stir together flours, sugar, walnuts and baking soda. Add to date mixture; stir just until flour mixture is moistened. Spoon mixture into prepared muffin cups. Bake in 375° oven 25 minutes or until golden brown. Immediately remove from pan. Cool on wire rack or serve warm.

Best Foods   **Englewood Cliffs, New Jersey**

Main Entrees
Beef, Lamb, Pork & Veal

Porcupine Meatballs

Serves 5 to 6

1½ lbs. ground beef
1 teaspoon salt
½ cup rice

½ teaspoon pepper
1 tablespoon onion, minced
1 can tomato soup
½ cup water

This is to be done in a pressure cooker. Wash rice. Combine meat, salt, rice, pepper, and onion. Shape into small balls. Heat tomato soup and water in cooker. Drop meatballs in soup mixture. Close cover securely. Place regulator on vent and cook, 10 minutes at 15 lbs. Let pressure drop before opening pan.

This recipe can be done in less than 30 minutes if cooked in a pressure pan. May be served over mashed potatoes.

Karen McCord   **Lindsay High School, Lindsay**

Meatballs in Gravy

Serves 6

2 lbs. ground beef
1 egg
½ cup dry seasoned bread crumbs
1 28 oz. can tomatoes
1 10 oz. can cream of
  mushroom soup

1 packet dry onion soup mix
1 tablespoon corn starch
1 tablespoon worchestershire or
  steak sauce

Combine and mix well the ground beef, egg and bread crumbs. Shape into meatballs and brown in a skillet. Combine in a 2 qt. saucepan the tomatoes, soup, dry soup mix, cornstarch and steak sauce. Add the browned meatballs and simmer about 30 minutes. Serve over rice, noodles or potatoes.

Carolyn Yeutter   **Norco Junior High School, Norco**

15 Minute Beef Stroganoff

Serves 2 to 4

1 lb. round or sirloin steak
2 tablespoons butter
8 oz. mushrooms, canned or fresh
½ cup water

1 package Lipton Onion Soup Mix
8 oz. carton sour cream
2 tablespoons flour
cooked noodles or rice

Slice beef in thin strips. Saute beef quickly in butter or margarine. Add canned mushrooms plus ½ cup water or if desired saute fresh mushrooms separately. Add onion soup mix and cook briefly to dissolve contents of package. Mix flour with sour cream. Add sour cream to meat mixture and heat through. Do not boil or sour cream may curdle. Do not add salt until you taste it. Serve over noodles or rice.

This works well with chicken also (breast meat cut in chunks). Sometimes I substitute white wine for all or part of water. So easy and so good. If you like California Dip, you'll love this one.

Diana Moniz   **Rancho Alamitos High School, Garden Grove**

Teriyaki for Sirloin Tip

Serves 4 to 6

½ cup brown sugar
½ cup white sugar
½ cup soy sauce

1 clove garlic, chopped
1 inch ginger, chopped
1½ lbs. sirloin tip,
    cut into thin slices

Mix the first 5 ingredients together. Put meat in a pan and pour the sauce over the top. Marinate over night. Fry or barbeque meat in a heavy skillet.

Serve over rice with pea pods and a salad.

Joretta Stewart   *Olive Junior High School, Baldwin Park*

Mom's Meatballs

Serves 4 to 6

1 lb. lean ground beef
1 egg, beaten
1 small can green chili salsa
1 cup bread crumbs

2 tablespoons parsley
¼ cup onion, minced
garlic salt to taste
salt and pepper to taste
2 cans beef consomme

Mix all ingredients in order given, except beef consomme. Shape into small balls and brown in skillet until almost done. Transfer meatballs to a baking dish and cover with beef consomme. Bake at 325° for 1 to 1½ hours.

This has become a real favorite at our family gatherings. If you are in a real hurry, you do not need to brown the meatballs prior to putting them in the oven.

Gerry Henderson   *Temple City High School, Temple City*

Delicious Steak Sauce

Yields 2½ cups

1 18 oz. jar French's Cattlemen's regular barbecue sauce
½ cup sugar
¾ cup soy sauce

Mix above ingredients and marinate meat overnight.

Linda Tsutsui   *Hanford Union High School, Hanford*

Marilyn's Beef Burgundy

2 lbs. stew meat, cut into bite size pieces
1 package dry onion soup mix
1 can cream of mushroom soup
½ cup burgundy

Mix together all ingredients and put in 2 quart covered casserole. Cook 2½ to 3 hours at 325°. Serve over rice or noodles.

Delicious!

Brenda Umbro   *San Marcos Junior High School, San Marcos*

Red Simmered Beef (Fukien Style)

Serves 6 to 8

3 lbs. beef (chuck), whole or cut into 1½ inch cubes
½ cup soy sauce
½ cup water
2 tablespoons brown sugar

Place meat into a heavy sauce pan or dutch oven. Mix soy sauce, sugar and water and add to meat. Cover and cook over low heat for ten minutes, turning meat once. Reduce heat and simmer, covered, until tender about 1½ to 2 hours for whole piece of meat and 1 hour for cubes.

Serve with steamed or fried rice.

Carol Lovett   *Ensign Middle School, Newport Beach*

Sweet and Saucy Beef

Serves 6

1½ lbs. boneless beef
½ onion, chopped

Sauce:

1 cup water   3 tablespoons vinegar
1 cup catsup   3 tablespoons worcestershire sauce
3 tablespoons soy sauce   ⅓ cup sugar

Dredge meat with flour, salt and pepper. Place in a casserole; add onion, cover with sauce. Bake in 300° oven for 3½ to 4 hours. Serve over rice.

Roberta S. Priestley   *Alhambra High School, Alhambra*

Silver Plated Pot Roast

Serves 4

Pot roast to serve 4   celery stalks
salt and pepper   carrots, sliced
                               onion, sliced

Sauce:

3 tablespoons flour   ¾ cup catsup
1 tablespoon brown sugar   ½ cup water
1 teaspoon salt and pepper   1½ tablespoon Worcestershire sauce
½ teaspoon dry mustard   1 teaspoon vinegar

Combine sauce ingredients in a bowl. Brown pot roast in oil. Season with salt and pepper. Prepare a double piece of foil large enough to cover roast and vegetables on top and bottom. On the bottom piece of foil pour ½ of the sauce mixture. Put pot roast onto sauce. On top of roast put the quantities of carrots, onions, and celery you desire. (6 carrots, 4 celery, 1 onion are recommended.) Pour remaining sauce over meat and vegetables. Wrap loosely with foil. Pierce foil on top to let a little steam escape. Bake at 350° for 3 hours. Serve over noodles.

Put a cookie sheet under foil package to catch any leaks; or avoid the foil and throw everything into your crockpot.

Ginny Loranger   *Luther Burbank Jr. High School, Burbank*

Alhambra High School
Moore Room BBQ Ribs

Serves 4

2 lbs. farmer style ribs
1/2 cup catsup
3 tablespoons worcestershire sauce
1 1/2 teaspoons chili powder

1/2 teaspoon salt
1 dash Tabasco sauce
1 cup water

Mix all ingredients in a pan and simmer for 5 minutes. Pour over spareribs; cover and bake at 325° for 2 hours.

This is one of the favorite dishes served in our R.O.P. restaurant on campus. Combined with baked potato (done in the oven during the last hour) and green salad, it's a great and easy meal.

Linda Hsieh   **Alhambra High School, Alhambra**

Steak Diane

Serves 4 to 6

1/4 cup butter or margarine
2 to 2 1/2 lbs. beef fillet or
  other tender boneless beef
  cut 1/2 inch thick
2 tablespoons fresh lemon juice

1 tablespoon worcestershire sauce
2 tablespoons parsley, chopped
2 tablespoons chives, chopped
parsley and lemon wedges
  for garnish

Over high heat melt butter or margarine. Put in meat and brown quickly on both sides; cook to desired doneness, about 3 to 6 minutes. Remove meat to heated platter. Add lemon juice, worcestershire, chives and parsley to the pan; stir together. Pour sauce at once over the steaks; garnish with parsley and lemon wedges.

Carol Lovett   **Ensign Middle School, Newport Beach**

Perfect Short Ribs

Serves 6

4 lbs. short ribs
salt
pepper
1 8 oz. can tomato sauce

2 tablespoons molasses
2 tablespoons cider vinegar
1 onion, sliced
1 teaspoon liquid smoke

Sprinkle the short ribs with salt and pepper. Place in a 9x13 inch baking pan. Mix all remaining ingredients together and pour over ribs. Cover tightly with aluminum foil. Bake at 250° for 5 to 6 hours.

Adrienne Steele   **Lee Junior High School, Woodland**

Oven Pot Roast

Serves 4 to 6

4 to 5 lb. chuck roast
1 package Lipton onion soup mix
1 can condensed cream of mushroom soup

Line a 13x9 inch baking pan with heavy duty aluminum foil. Place chuck roast in pan. Sprinkle in onion soup mix. Spread on cream of mushroom soup. Wrap tightly in foil. Bake at 325° for 3 to 3½ hours.

On real hectic days I assemble this with a FROZEN pot roast in the morning and leave it in my oven on "time cook" and when I get home my dinner is ready.

Linda Hsieh   **Alhambra High School, Alhambra**

Special Hamburger (or Meatloaf)

Serves 3

⅓ cup evaporated milk	**Piquant Sauce**
2 tablespoons dried minced onions	
1 teaspoon salt	*3 tablespoons brown sugar*
¼ teaspoon pepper	*¼ cup catsup*
1/8 teaspoon nutmeg	*¼ teaspoon nutmeg*
¼ teaspoon garlic powder	*1 teaspoon dry mustard*
1 lb. ground beef	

Put everything but the beef into a bowl; leave for 5 minutes so onions will re-hydrate with the milk. Add beef and mix well with your hands. Shape into 3 patties or a meatloaf. Hamburgers may be charcoaled, pan fried or broiled to desired degree of doneness. Bake meatloaf at 350° for about 45 minutes. Hamburgers may be shaped like donuts, with a hole in the center and oven broiled at 500° for about 5 minutes. Mix piquant sauce and spread on donut-shaped burgers; turn the oven to 450° BAKE. Bake for 10 more minutes without turning.

I usually make this in 3 pound batches and freeze the uncooked extra.

Polly Frank   **Lakewood High School, Lakewood**

A Not-Mother's Chili

Serves 10 to 12

2 lbs. hamburger	*2 cups water*
4 medium large onions, diced	*1 clove garlic, minced*
4 cans 15 oz. kidney beans	*3 teaspoons chili powder*
4 cans condensed tomato soup	
(undiluted)	

Cook the hamburger and onions in a large pan until the hamburger is browned. Add the rest of the ingredients and cook slowly, stirring occasionally, for about 3 hours.

When I was growing up, we always had a big kettle of this for friends who stopped at our house after University of Iowa football games.

Polly Frank   **Lakewood High School, Lakewood**

Taco Burgers

Serves 4

1 lb. ground beef
1 16 oz. can tomatoes
1 package taco seasoning mix
4 hamburger buns, split and toasted
1 cup cheddar cheese, shredded
2 cups lettuce, shredded

Brown beef until crumbly; drain. Add tomatoes and seasoning mix. Stir well, breaking up large pieces of tomato. Bring to boiling; reduce heat and simmer 10 minutes. Spoon meat over buns and sprinkle cheese and lettuce on top.

Penny Niadna   *Golden West High School, Visalia*

California Spring Lamb

Serves 6 to 8

1 leg spring lamb,
cut into 2 inch cubes
1 onion, cut into quarters
½ cup oil
1 bell pepper, cut into 1 inch pieces

2 cups wine
1 cup soy sauce
1 tablespoon garlic salt
1 tablespoon parsley, chopped

Combine all ingredients in large covered container. Marinate for 24 hours. Arrange lamb cubes and vegetables on skewers and barbeque. Choose vegetables that please family taste.

Serve with rice pilaf and green salad for a fast and tasty meal.

Sally Oxford   **Monache High School, Porterville**

Roast Rack of Lamb

Serves 4

2 racks of spring lamb, trimmed
(about 1½ lbs. each)
1 teaspoon thyme

Salt and freshly ground pepper
1 teaspoon vegetable oil
½ cup dry white wine

Preheat the oven to 450°. Season the lamb with the thyme and salt and pepper to taste. Place in a roasting pan and sprinkle the oil over the meat. Roast for 30 to 40 minutes, according to taste. (Rack of lamb is best when quite pink.) The lamb should be rare after 30 minutes, medium after 35 minutes and well done after 40 minutes. Transfer the roasted lamb to a serving platter. Discard all but 1 tablespoon of the drippings from the pan. Deglaze the pan with the white wine. Pour the juices over the lamb, carve and serve.

Serve with a bibb lettuce salad, wild rice and baby carrots.

Nan Paul   **Grant School, Escondido**

Barbecued Pork Chops

Serves 4

1 cup catsup
⅓ cup worcestershire sauce
1 teaspoon chili powder
1 teaspoon salt
¼ cup onion, chopped (optional)

½ cup bell pepper, chopped
(optional)
8 wafer thin sliced pork chops
1 large onion, cut in 8 slices
1 lemon, cut in 8 slices

Combine first 6 ingredients in pyrex bowl; cook on high in microwave oven for 5 minutes. Meanwhile, trim fat from pork chops with kitchen shears; brown in electric skillet at 400°. Turn. Place onion slices, then lemon slices on top. Cover with barbecue sauce; place lid on pan and simmer at 300 to 350° for 30 minutes or until sauce is reduced and somewhat thickened. Remove lid in the last 10 to 15 minutes cooking period.

Serve with home fries, frozen broccoli and applesauce.

Ellie Wildermuth   **La Canada High School, La Canada**

Southern Ham & Sweet Potatoes Ⓜ

Serves 6

2 cups cooked ham, diced
2 cups peas or 1 #2 can
1 can condensed mushroom soup
1 29 oz. can sweet potatoes, drained

2 tablespoons butter
¼ teaspoon salt
½ teaspoon cinnamon

Combine cooked ham, peas and soup in greased 1½ quart casserole. Mash sweet potatoes; add butter, salt and cinnamon. Place sweet potato mixture in mounds on top of ham mixture in casserole. Bake in moderate oven 350° for 20 minutes or in microwave in casserole dish with covering for 3 minutes turn ¼ turn and bake another 3 minutes at #1 high temperature.

This recipe is good to use with leftover ham or any cooked ham.

Elda G. Benson   *Corona Junior High School, Corona*

Peachy Keen Pork Chops

Serves 6 to 8

1 egg, slightly beaten
¼ cup milk
¼ cup parmesan cheese
1 package Mrs. Cubbison's
   dressing mix
6 to 8 ¾ inch pork chops
salt and pepper

6 to 8 peach halves, drained
   (saving juice)

Peach sauce:
½ cup peach juice
¼ cup brown sugar
½ teapsoon ground ginger

Mix egg and milk. Mix parmesan cheese and dressing mix. Coat pork chops into egg mixture (both sides) and then into dressing mixture. Salt and pepper to taste. Brown chops on both sides in lightly oiled skillet. Arrange in baking dish with peach halves. Baste peaches with sauce periodically during baking. Bake 45 to 50 minutes in 350° oven.

June Muraoka   *Cypress High School, Cypress*

Quick Sweet and Sour Pork

Serves 4

2 tablespoons corn oil
1 lb. boneless pork,
   cut into 2 inch cubes
1 15¼ oz. can pineapple chunks
½ cup dark Karo corn syrup
¼ cup vinegar

2 tablespoons catsup
2 tablespoons soy sauce
1 clove garlic, minced
2 tablespoons cornstarch
2 tablespoons water
½ cup green pepper,
   cut into 1 inch pieces

Heat corn oil in skillet. Brown pork. Add the next 6 ingredients. Bring ingredients to a boil, then turn down and simmer for 10 minutes. Mix cornstarch with 2 tablespoons water; add to pork mixture. Add green pepper. Simmer 2 minutes, stirring constantly. Serve over steamed rice.

Pat Smith   *Kern Valley High School, Lake Isabella*

Saucy Pork

3 to 4 pork steaks
1 can golden mushroom soup
1 can cream of celery soup
½ to ¾ cup milk
1 small onion, sliced very thin

Place pork in baking dish. Mix soup together and add ½ to ¾ can milk and onions. Pour sauce over pork and place in center of oven. Bake 350° for about 45 minutes or until pork is thoroughly baked. Serve over brown rice.

Judi Topp   *Raney Junior High School, Corona*

Moo Shu Pork

Serves 4

1 lb. ground pork	1 teaspoon sugar
1 small onion	salt and pepper to taste
2 tablespoons oil	2 teaspoons cornstarch
½ head cabbage (2 cups)	2 tablespoons water
3 tablespoons soy sauce	8 flour tortillas
¼ cup water	¼ cup Chinese Plum Sauce

Brown the onion and pork in 2 tablespoons oil. Cook until meat is no longer pink. Drain off fat. Add the cabbage and stir fry for 5 minutes. Add soy sauce and water, sugar and seasonings and cook until vegetables are soft. Thicken the gravy with the mixture of cornstarch and water. Serve in heated flour tortilla with 1 teaspoon plum sauce in the middle.

Sylvia Hayashi   *Crescent Valley High School, La Crescenta*

Sausage Jambalaya

Serves 4 to 6

1 cup instant rice	*1 medium onion, chopped*
(regular may be used)	*½ cup green pepper, chopped*
1 lb. smoked sausage	*½ cup celery, sliced*
(cut into 2 inch pieces)	*1 8 oz. can stewed tomatoes*

Cook rice according to package directions. While rice is cooking, heat sausage. Add onion, green pepper and celery and saute until vegetables are tender. Add tomatoes. Drain cooked rice and stir into sausage mixture. Cook over low heat, stirring frequently, until thoroughly heated. If you like hot spicy food, add 4 drops of hot pepper sauce and ¼ teaspoon pepper.

To save time bake meat loaf in muffin tins. It only takes 15 minutes.

Betty M. Williams   *East Bakersfield High School, Bakersfield*

Veal Parmegiana

Serves 4

½ cup corn flakes
¼ cup grated parmesan cheese
½ teaspoon salt / dash of pepper
1 lb. veal cutlets (¼ inch thick)
1 egg, slightly beaten
3 tablespoons butter or margarine

1 8 oz. can tomato sauce
½ teaspoon oregano, crushed
½ teaspoon sugar
dash onion salt
2 thin slices mozzarella cheese,
  4 oz. halved

Preheat oven to 400°. Grease or Pam 10x6x1½ inch baking dish. Combine corn flake crumbs, parmesan cheese, salt and pepper. Cut veal in serving pieces; dip in egg then in crumb mixture. In large skillet place the butter and melt over medium heat. Place breaded veal in skillet and brown on both sides about 15 minutes and then place in baking dish. Meanwhile, combine tomato sauce, oregano, sugar and onion salt in a small sauce pan. Heat to boiling, stirring frequently. Reduce heat to low until all meat is browned. Pour sauce over meat. Top with cheese. Place in oven to melt and slightly brown cheese, about 15 minutes.

Serve with egg noodles (parsley), green salad and soudough bread. The pre-formed veal patties in the freezer section at the market work excellently and do not have to be defrosted. Just add more time when browning the meat.

Marie Humphrey
                                          Grant School, Escondido

Veal Oscar

Serves 4

1 lb. fresh veal scallopini
  (thin sliced veal)
salt and pepper to taste
½ pound crab legs or pieces

1 pound fresh asparagus
  (can substitute broccoli)
1 can hollandaise sauce
¼ cup butter

Saute veal in 2 tablespoons butter until done. Season with salt and pepper and set aside. Saute crab in 2 tablespoons butter until warm. At the same time, steam asparagus or microwave until tender. Place hollandaise sauce in pan and warm or microwave 1 minute. Place cooked veal on platter or plate, top with crab, then asparagus, and hollandaise sauce on top. Garnish with parsley.

Great, easy, can be completed in less than 20 minutes!

Elizabeth Bruce
                                     Troy High School, Fullerton

Veal Piccata

Serves 2 to 4

4 pieces scaloppine of veal
2 tablespoons flour
4 tablespoons margarine

1 clove garlic
¼ cup dry vermouth
1 tablespoon lemon juice
½ lemon, sliced

Pound veal with wooden mallet to 1/8 inch. Dredge in flour; shake off excess. In skillet, melt 3 tablespoons margarine. Crush garlic and brown. Discard clove. Place veal in skillet and cook quickly 1 to 2 minutes each side. Remove to warm serving dish. Add 1 tablespoon margarine, wine, and lemon juice. Simmer 5 minutes, scraping bottom of pan to loosen drippings. Pour over veal. Garnish with lemon slices.

Sharletta Kay Myers   *DeMille Junior High School, Long Beach*

Main Entrees
Poultry

Janice's Curry Chicken

Serves 2 to 3

½ cup mayonnaise
½ cup milk
1 can cream of mushroom soup

curry powder to taste
1 package chicken drummettes

Mix mayonnaise, milk, soup and curry powder together. Place chicken drummettes in baking pan that has been greased. Pour curry mixture over chicken. Cover with foil and bake in 350° oven for 45 minutes to 1 hour.

Linda Tsutsui   *Hanford Union High School, Hanford*

Chicken Supreme

Serves 10 to 12

5 to 6 whole chicken breasts,
   halved and skinned
1 can whole cranberry sauce

1 package dry onion soup mix
1 small bottle Creamy Orange
   French dressing

Place chicken breasts in a 9x13 inch pan. Mix ingredients and pour over chicken breasts. Cover with foil and bake at 350° for 1 hour. It's better if reheated and served the next day.

This is super quick and easy and delicious served with rice and a green salad.

Phyllis Kaylor   *Ray A. Kroc Middle School, San Diego*

Dijon Chicken

Serves 4 to 6

2 chickens, quartered
1 8 oz. bottle Italian Dressing
2 green onions, chopped

2 tablespoons Dijon mustard
¼ cup dry white wine

Place chicken, skin side down, in a shallow baking pan, Combine all ingredients and pour over chicken. Cover dish and refrigerate 24 hours. Next day: Turn chicken, skin side up, and bake at 350° *for 1 to 1½ hours. Or barbeque chicken and baste with the sauce.*

Katie Morrison-Gold   *Olive Peirce Junior High school, Ramona*

Simply Chicken

Serves 4

4 chicken breasts, skinned
1 jar (can) Italian sauce or sweet and sour sauce
Jack Cheese, grated (optional)

Place skinned chicken in baking dish. Pour sauce over chicken and bake 350° until chicken is tender (about 30 minutes). Grate cheese and add to dish last five minutes of cooking time.

Serve over bed of rice. Garnish platter with fresh steamed broccoli and mushrooms. If fewer servings are desired, use about ½ cup sauce per chicken breast.

Judi Topp   *Raney Junior High School, Corona*

Chicken 'N' Beef

Serves 6

1 package chipped beef
6 boneless chicken breasts
½ pound bacon

1 can cream of mushroom soup
1 large sour cream
2 to 4 tablespoons white wine
paprika

Lay chipped beef in bottom of 13x9 inch pan. Put skinned, boneless chicken breasts on top of beef. Cover with bacon (don't cool). Mix soup, sour cream and wine. Pour over top. Sprinkle with paprika. Bake 3 hours at 275°.

My family has used this recipe for years. It's so easy to put together. Most everyone thinks you've spent hours on this!

Dorothy Wilson   *Dale Junior High School, Anaheim*

One Pan Chicken and Rice

Serves 6 to 8

2 cups uncooked rice
1 can cream of mushroom soup
1 can chicken gumbo soup
1 soup can water

1 package Lipton dry onion soup
2 cup up frying chickens
(may omit wings and backs)

Mix rice, the 2 cans of soup and one can of water in the 12x18 inch baking pan. (Or use one 9x13 inch and 1 8x8 inch pan, splitting up the ingredients.) Shake up package of onion soup mix in package before opening and press with fingers to mix ingredients in package, then sprinkle ¼ of package over mixture. Skin chicken and place on top of mixture, then sprinkle rest of onion soup mix on top of chicken. Cover with foil and bake at 350° for about 2 hours. Uncover the last 15 minutes.

This is so easy yet the chicken gumbo soup makes it different than any other recipes I've tried.

Glenell Fuller   *Glendora High School, Glendora*

Chicken Divan

Serves 6 to 8

2 10 oz. packages of frozen broccoli, thawed
3 cups cooked chicken breasts
2 10½ oz. cans cream of chicken soup
¾ cup mayonnaise or Miracle Whip
1 teaspoon lemon juice
2 cups sharp cheddar cheese, grated
1 cup seasoned bread crumbs
2 tablespoons butter, melted

Butter 9x13 inch casserole dish. Arrange broccoli in dish, then add cooked chicken. Combine soup, mayonnaise and lemon juice. Pour over broccoli and chicken. Sprinkle cheese and bread crumbs on top. Drizzle with butter. Bake one hour at 350°.

May be frozen.

Lois Armstrong   *Sonora High School, La Habra*

Parmesan Chicken

Serves 4 to 6

2 cups bread crumbs
¾ cup parmesan cheese
¼ cup parsley, chopped
¼ teaspoon garlic powder

2 teaspoons salt
½ teaspoon pepper
1 cube margarine or butter
4 to 6 chicken breasts

Mix 2 cups of bread crumbs with parmesan cheese, parsley, garlic powder, salt and pepper. Melt the margarine or butter. Remove the skin from the chicken pieces and dip them into the margarine and then the crumb mixture. Arrange the chicken in a shallow pan that has been lined with foil. Do not overlap pieces. Bake 1 hour at 350°.

Great for a company dinner that's casual.

Beverly Fincher-Ranger   **Carpinteria High School, Carpinteria**

Curry Chicken

Serves 4 to 6

3 full boned chicken breasts
2 cans cream of chicken soup
1 cup mayonnaise
1 tablespoon lemon juice

1 teaspoon curry powder
½ cup mild cheddar cheese, grated
½ cups cracker crumbs,
  browned in butter

Dredge chicken in flour and brown in butter. Place in greased baking dish and cover with mixture of soup, mayonnaise, lemon juice and curry powder. Sprinkle with cheese then cracker crumbs. Bake at 350° for 30 to 45 minutes.

A very mild lemony-curry flavored dish everyone likes.

Mrs. Linda Robinson   **Sinaloa Junior High School, Simi Valley**

Chicken Perfection

Serves 2 to 4

4 single chicken breasts,
  boned and skinned
⅓ cup flour
¼ cup vegetable oil
½ cup onion, chopped or sliced

1 large lemon, sliced paper thin
1 tablespoon instant chicken bouillon
1 cup hot water
4 springs parsley, snipped
  (for garnish)

Pound each breast to ¼ inch thickness with a meat mallet. Coat each piece of chicken in flour. Saute the chicken over medium heat in a 10 inch frying pan for 2½ minutes on each side. Remove chicken from pan and drain on brown paper. Add onion to pan and saute 1 to 2 minutes. Remove and drain. Pour off excess oil from the pan. Return chicken and onion to the pan; top with lemon slices. Mix bouillon and 1 cup of hot water and pour over chicken. Cover and simmer for 5 minutes. Arrange chicken on platter and garnish with parsley.

This chicken is so tender you can cut it with a fork.

Joanne Toone-Cooper   **Hamilton Junior High School, Long Beach**

Tarragon Chicken

Serves 4

4 boneless chicken breasts
1 tablespoon flour
½ teaspoon dried tarragon, crushed
2 tablespoons margarine

⅓ cup hot water
1 teaspoon instant chicken bouillon
1 teaspoon lemon juice
parsley, snipped

Cut boned chicken breast halves into ½ inch wide strips. Combine flour and tarragon in a small paper bag; add chicken pieces and shake to coat. In 10 inch skillet, melt margarine and saute chicken over medium high heat for 5 to 6 minutes, turning chicken pieces often. Combine hot water, chicken bouillon granules and lemon juice; add to skillet. Stir, scraping up browned particles. Cover and simmer for 3 to 4 minutes. Sprinkle with parsley before serving.

Takes approximately 25 minutes total preparation. Great with rice and a tossed salad.

Madalyn Seguin   **Venado Middle School, Irvine**

Chicken Cordon Bleu

Serves 4

1 whole chicken breast, boned
   and split into fourths
4 slices ham

4 slices Swiss cheese
1 egg beaten
seasoned bread crumbs

Remove the skin and the bone from the chicken breast. Pound each quarter section of chicken thinly between two sheets of waxpaper. Be careful not to tear chicken. (Use rolling pin to pound.) Cover each section with a slice of ham and of cheese and roll up. Secure with toothpicks. Dip each roll in egg and then in bread crumbs. Saute in melted butter in frying pan or bake in a 350° oven until done.

Very quick to fix if chicken breasts are purchased with the bone removed. It's an attractive and tasty entree.

Bonnie Pius   **Sanger High School, Sanger**

Chicken Enchiladas

2 to 3 dozen tortillas
2 cups cooked chicken
   approximately
3 to 4 cups cheddar cheese,
   shredded

1 cup onions, chopped (optional)
2 cans cream of chicken soup
1 pint sour cream
1 4 oz. can diced green chiles

Place a small amount of chicken lengthwise in the center of each tortilla, follow with some grated cheese and onion. Roll up each tortilla and place in a baking pan. Continue until all tortillas are used. Mix remaining ingredients (soup, sour cream, chiles) and spread over top of tortillas. Cover with remaining cheese. Bake at 350° for 20 to 25 minutes.

If tortillas are not soft enough to roll easily, they can be dipped in hot oil to soften or layered (stacked) in a casserole dish.

Leonda Lines   **Leuzinger High School, Lawndale**

Chicken Wings With Lime Butter

Serves 4

20 chicken wings.
½ teaspoon salt
½ teaspoon pepper
⅓ cup cooking oil

1 lime, juiced
8 tablespoons butter
½ teaspoon chives, minced
½ teaspoon dill weed

Sprinkle chicken on both sides with salt and pepper. In fry pan heat oil to medium temperature. Add chicken and saute about 4 minutes or until lightly brown. Turn chicken; cover and reduce heat to low. Cook 10 minutes or until fork tender. Remove chicken and keep warm; drain off oil. In same fry pan, add lime juice and cook over low heat until juice begins to bubble. Add butter, stirring until butter becomes opaque and forms a thickened sauce. Stir in chives and dill weed. Spoon sauce over chicken.

Eudora Mitchell   *Norwalk High School, Norwalk*

Parisian Chicken Marengo

Serves 8

4 chicken breasts, halved
¼ cup flour
1 teaspoon paprika
½ teaspoon salt
¼ teaspoon pepper
5 tablespoons butter or margarine
¾ cup white wine

1 3 oz. can button mushrooms
1 10½ oz. can cream of chicken
 soup
¼ cup currant jelly
¼ cup green onions, sliced
½ tablespoon brown bouquet sauce
1/8 teaspoon tabasco sauce

Coat chicken with combined flour, paprika, salt and pepper. Brown in hot butter in electric skillet set at 300° (medium heat). Pour combined remaining ingredients over chicken. Cover, turn dial to 210° (simmer heat); cook 30 minutes or until tender. Serve over noodles or rice.

Excellent the next day. Can be frozen and reheated.

Andrea Roberts   *Meadowbrook Middle School, Poway*

Chicken Piccata

Serves 4 to 6

3 whole chicken breasts
3 tablespoons butter or margarine
1 tablespoon flour
1 teaspoon salt

1 teaspoon dried leaf tarragon
½ cup chicken broth
3 thin lemon slices, halved
1 teaspoon parsley, minced

Bone and skin chicken breasts, then cut into halves. Melt butter in large skillet. Add chicken. Sprinkle with flour, salt and tarragon. Cook and stir 5 minutes. Add chicken broth and lemon slices. Stir chicken to loosen any browned particles. Cover and cook another 5 minutes, or until chicken breasts are done, over low heat. Serve over rice or pasta if desired. Sprinkle with minced parsley.

Easy, fast and low calorie!

Jan Hirth   *Saddleback High School, Santa Ana*

Fila Chicken Packets

Serves 6

¾ cup green onion, chopped
¾ cup mayonnaise
3 tablespoons lemon juice
3 cloves, garlic, minced or pressed
¾ teaspoons dry tarragon

⅔ cup butter or margarine
12 sheets fila
6 boneless chicken breasts,
   halved and skinned
salt and pepper to taste
2 tablespoons parmesan cheese

Mix together green onion, mayonnaise, lemon juice, 2 cloves of the garlic, and the tarragon, set aside. Combine remaining garlic with the butter. For each packet, place 1 sheet of fila on a board and brush it with about 2 teaspoons garlic butter; arrange a second sheet on top and brush it with another 2 teaspoons garlic butter. Lightly sprinkle a chicken piece with salt and pepper. Spoon about 3 tablespoons of herb mayonnaise over both sides of chicken breast. Place onto corner of fila. Flip corner of fila over chicken; roll once. Fold sides in; then roll up to opposite corner. Place the 6 packets slightly apart in an ungreased baking pan. Brush with remaining garlic butter; sprinkle with cheese. Bake in a 375° oven for 20 to 25 minutes or until golden. Serve hot.

This is an easy, yet elegant dish. Leftovers reheat beautifully. To make ahead, freeze before cooking. Pack in a single layer in a container with tight fitting lid. Thaw completely; cover before baking.

Susan Roa Hope   **Lompoc Valley Middle School, Lompoc**

Sweet and Sour Chicken

Serves 6

½ bottle Russian salad dressing
1 envelope onion soup mix

½ cup apricot/pineapple jam
1 chicken, cut up

Mix ingredients. Pour over chicken. Bake uncovered in a 350° oven for 45 minutes.

Serve remaining sauce over white rice.

Joyce Grohmann   **Bellflower High School, Bellflower**

Chicken Curry

Serves 4

½ cup honey
½ cup Dijon mustard
scant tablespoon curry powder

2 tablespoons soy sauce
8 chicken breasts

Mix all ingredients well and pour over chicken breasts. Marinate all day or overnight. Bake 350° for 1 hour.

Barb Gibbons   **Harbour View School, Huntington Beach**

Chicken and Dressing

Serves 8

1 cooked chicken
onion and celery, sliced (to taste)
salt and pepper (to taste)
1 package Pepperidge Farm dressing
2 cans cream of mushroom soup

Cook chicken by simmering, covered, in water with sliced onion, sliced celery, salt and pepper until tender. Cool and remove meat from bones. Mix dressing according to package directions, using broth from cooking the chicken instead of water. Arrange in casserole with one layer dressing, one layer chicken, one layer soup. Repeat. Bake 350° for 45 minutes.

Lorraine Pepper   *Oceanside High School, Oceanside*

Day-After Divan

Serves 4

1 10 oz. package frozen broccoli or asparagus spears, cooked and drained
4 large slices chicken or turkey
1 10½ oz. can cream of chicken, celery or mushroom soup
⅓ cup milk
½ cup cheddar cheese, shredded

Arrange broccoli in shallow 10x6x2 inch baking dish. Top with turkey slices. Blend soup and milk, pour over turkey. Sprinkle with cheese. Bake at 450° until sauce is slightly browned, about 15 minutes.

Great for holiday leftovers.

Gloria Walker   *Casa Roble Fundamental High School, Orangevale*

Oriental Chicken Buns

Serves 5

2 tablespoons sugar
1 to 1½ teaspoons fresh
  ginger root, finely grated
1 clove garlic, minced
2 tablespoons soy sauce
2 boned chicken breasts, cut into
  ½ inch cubes (1½ cups)
2 teaspoons cornstarch

1 tablespoon water
⅓ cup water chestnuts,
  finely chopped
1 green onon, chopped
10 oz. can Hungry Jack®
  Refrigerated Flaky biscuits
1 to 2 tablespoons margarine,
  melted
sesame seed

Heat oven to 375°F. In medium skillet, combine sugar, ginger, garlic and soy sauce. Cook over medium heat until boiling; add chicken. Cook 3 to 4 minutes or until chicken becomes opaque; remove from heat. With a slotted spoon, remove chicken from ginger liquid; drain well reserving ginger liquid. Combine cornstarch and water; stir into reserved ginger liquid. Return to heat; heat to boiling, stirring continuously. Cook until clear and thickened. Stir in chicken mixture, water chestnuts and green onion. Remove from heat; cool 10 minutes.

Separate dough into 10 biscuits; press or roll each biscuit to 4 inch circle. Place 2 tablespoons chicken mixture on center of each piece of dough. Fold dough over chicken, covering completely. Seal well; shape into balls. Place filled biscuits seam side down on ungreased cookie sheet. Brush tops with margarine; sprinkle with sesame seed. Bake at 375°F. for 9 to 14 minutes or until golden brown. Remove from cookie sheet immediately.

TIP: To reheat, wrap loosely in foil; heat at 350°F. for 14 to 16 minutes.

The Pillsbury Company   **Minneapolis, Minnesota**

Main Entrees

Seafood

Recipe for "Shrimp Saute" on page 66

Chopstick Tuna

Serves 4

1 can cream of mushroom soup
¼ cup water
1 3 oz. can chow mein noodles
1 6 oz. can tuna

1 cup celery, sliced
½ cup cashews
½ cup onion, finely chopped
¼ oz. can mandarin oranges,
    drained

Combine all ingredients EXCEPT ½ cup noodles and mandarin oranges. Put in ungreased 7x10 inch baking dish. Sprinkle reserved noodles over top. Bake at 375° for 15 minutes. Garnish with mandarin oranges.

Penny Niadna   *Golden West High School, Visalia*

Spanish Clam Parmesan

Serves 4

2 tablespoons olive oil
2 tablespoons butter
1 large onion, chopped
1 teaspoon salt
1 teaspoon pepper

2 tablespoons flour
1 8 oz. can minced clams
1 package chopped spinach,
    defrosted
½ cup Parmesan cheese

Combine oil and butter in a frying pan. Saute onion in above mixture with salt and pepper and flour. Add clam juice, stir, add clams, stir and add defrosted spinach plus ¼ cup of the parmesan cheese. Pour mixture into a casserole dish. Sprinkle with remaining cheese. Bake 325° for 30 minutes.

Marianne Traw   *Ball Junior High School, Anaheim*

Shrimp Casserole

Serves 6

1 bunch fresh spinach
1 can all natural spinach
    Campbell's soup
½ cup salsa
½ lb. fresh mushrooms
1 large onion

3 tablespoons butter
¾ lb. shrimp
Corn tortillas
½ lb. cheddar cheese, grated
1 small can olives

Wash spinach and break into bite size pieces; let drain. Heat soup in sauce pan. Add salsa. Put aside on low burner to keep warm. Wash mushrooms. Chop onion and mushrooms and put in fry pan with butter and saute. Add soup mixture. Wash shrimp, put in fry pan and more butter, if needed; saute 5 to 6 minutes. Add soup to mixture. Add fresh spinach just before layering. Grease casserole dish. Break corn tortillas into bite size pieces and layer bottom of dish. Layer ingredients as follows: corn tortillas, filling, cheese, corn tortillas, filling, cheese and olives. Put under broiler 10 minutes or until cheese is melted and casserole is warm.

May be garnished with either avocado or sour cream. Any protein food may be substituted for shrimp; i.e., chicken, beef, crab, etc.

Jackie Brodwolf   *Helix High School, La Mesa*

Seafood-Cheese Bake

Serves 6 to 8

10 oz. fetticini noodles
1 cup sharp cheese, shredded
1 family size can tuna, waterpacked
10 oz.can tiny shrimp
½ cup onion, chopped
½ cup green pepper, diced

½ cup red pepper, diced
1 teaspoon salt
1½ to 2 cans cream of celery soup
½ cup milk
½ cup slivered almonds

Cook noodles in salted water. Drain. Add grated cheese, blending until melted into noodles. Add all other ingredients. Place slivered almonds on top. Bake in 8 inch square casserole at 400° for 30 minutes.

Easy and inexpensive — A sure hit every time. I usually have diced onions and peppers in freezer — saves time when assembling the casserole. All other ingredients are things I always have on hand; so when unexpected guests pop in, this recipe is my 'standby'!

Helene Palmer   **Crescenta Valley High School, La Crescenta**

Savory Stuffed Trout ⓜ

Serves 2 to 4

2 whole cleaned trout,
   8 to 10 oz. each
2 tablespoons margarine
¼ cup green onions
½ cup carrots, grated

¼ cup zucchini
1 tablespoon fresh parsley, minced
¼ cup fine bread crumbs
¼ cup margarine, melted
2 tablespoons lemon juice

Arrange trout in 12x9 inch glass dish. Microwave 2 to 3 minutes or until bones may be removed. Put margarine, onions, carrots, zucchini and parsley in 2 cup glass measurer. Microwave on high 3 minutes. Stir in dry bread crumbs. Pack mixture in cavity of each trout. Pierce skin with knife. Mix margarine and lemon juice. Brush fish. Cover lightly with waxpaper. Microwave on high 5 to 8 minutes until fish flakes. Let stand 5 minutes.

Barbara Block   **Newport Harbor High School, Newport Beach**

Seafood Bean Casserole

Serves 5 to 6

½ cup milk
1 can cream of mushroom soup
1 teaspoon soy sauce
dash of pepper or hot sauce
2 16 oz. French cut green beans
   (or 3 cups frozen)

1 3 oz. can French fried onions
1 16 oz. package shrimp,
or 11 oz. can crab,
or leftover meat, chicken
Toast points or
1 16 oz. can chow mein noodles

In 1½ quart casserole, stir milk, soup, seasonings, until smooth. Mix in green beans, ½ of onions (save ½ for topping) and seafood. Bake 25 minutes or until hot at 350°. Sprinkle rest of onions on top. Bake 5 more minutes or leave as is. Serve on toast, chow mein noodles, rice or noodles.

Millie Walls   **El Dorado High School, Placentia**

China Poot's Best Halibut

Serves 4

1 10 oz. package chopped spinach
2 lbs. raw halibut
1 can cream of celery soup
½ cup mayonnaise or sour cream
½ teaspoon mustard

2 tablespoons lemon juice
½ teaspoon basil
2 tablespoons parsley
1 cup cheese, grated
    your preference of type of cheese

Spread thawed, drained spinach on bottom of buttered casserole dish. Flake the raw halibut and spread on top of spinach. Blend all remaining ingredients except the cheese and spread on top of the fish. Top it off with the cheese. Bake at 350° about 30 minutes or until cheese bubbles. Garnish and serve.

May vary the fish or use a combination for some variety.

Julie Hampton   **Franklin Junior High School, Long Beach**

Wine-Poached Halibut

Serves 6

3 large halibut steaks, each about
    1 pound and 1¼ inch thick
½ cup dry white wine or
    regular strength chicken broth
3 tablespoons lemon juice

4 tablespoons butter or margarine
½ cup green onion, thinly sliced
    (including tops)
salt and pepper

Cut halibut steaks in half lengthwise along center bone; discard bone. Arrange the 6 portions side by side in a greased 9x13 inch baking pan; pour in wine and lemon juice. Cover tightly with foil and bake at 375° for 15 to 20 minutes or until flesh inside is just opaque at thickest portion of fish. Lift fish from pan; arrange on platter and keep warm. Add butter and onions to juices in pan; place pan over medium high heat and bring butter mixture to a boil, stirring occasionally until reduced to ½ cup. Season to taste with salt and pepper and spoon over fish.

Kathie Baczynski   **Mt. Carmel High School, San Diego**

Salmon Bake

Serves 4 to 6

1 large can red salmon
1 small onion
1 tablespoon butter

1 tablespoon flour
1 cup milk
1 cup crushed saltine crackers

Drain salmon. Remove bones and skin. Flake salmon with fork. Set aside in a bowl. Dice small onion. Saute onion in 1 tablespoon butter over low heat about 5 minutes. Stir into butter a tablespoon of flour. Let mixture bubble about 1 minute. Gradually add 1 cup milk. Cook until white sauce has thickened on low heat. Add to salmon. Toss ingredients together. Butter a 2 to 2½ quart casserole dish. Line the bottom of baking dish with about ½ cup of crushed saltine crackers. Pour in salmon mixture. Top with remaining crushed crackers. Bake 400° oven for 30 minutes.

Carolyn Crum   **Newhart Junior High School, Mission Viejo**

Fillets Elegante

Serves 4

1 lb. frozen fish fillets
2 tablespoons butter
1 cup cheese sauce
  (make your own)

1 4½ to 5 oz. can shrimp, drained
¼ cup parmesan cheese, grated
paprika

Thaw fillets (sole, haddock, or halibut). Arrange in buttered 9 inch pie plate. Dash with pepper; dot wth butter. Prepare your cheese sauce and stir in shrimp. Spread cheese sauce with shrimp over fish. Sprinkle with parmesan cheese and paprika. Bake 400° for 20 minutes. Serve with lemon wedges.

Great!

Donna Goble   **Almondale School, Littlerock**

Lemon Pepper Fish (Low Fat)

Serves 1 or more

White fish (halibut or orange roughy)
1 to 2 tablespoons butter
Lemon (fresh or powder concentrate)
pepper

Preheat oven to 325°. Melt butter in baking dish. Coat fish in butter. Sprinkle one side with lemon and pepper . Bake for 10 to 15 minutes (depending on the thickness of fish). Turn and sprinkle second side with lemon and pepper. Finish baking. Fish should be moist and flaky. Do not overcook.

Orange Roughy bakes faster so you may need to reduce baking time.

Judi Topp   **Raney Junior High School, Corona**

Shrimp-Pea Salad

Serves 6 to 8

1 16 oz. package Petite Peas, frozen
½ lb. large shrimp, cooked
½ large purple onion
½ cup Best Foods mayonnaise

Drain peas in a collander. Pat dry. Cut shrimp into bit size pieces. Finely chop purple onion. Place the above ingredients in a medium bowl. Add mayonnaise and mix thoroughly.

Tess Osborne   **Columbus Tustin Intermediate School, Tustin**

Paella California Style

Serves 4

4 6 oz. Italian sausage rings
2 19 oz. cans minestrone soup
1 8 oz. can tomato sauce
½ to 1 teaspoon garlic powder

3 to 4 cooked chicken breasts,
  cut in bite sizes
1 to 2 cans medium to large shrimp
1½ cups minute rice, uncooked

Brown sausage pieces on both sides. Add soup, sauce, and garlic powder. Bring to the boiling point. Simmer 2 to 3 minutes. Add cooked chicken pieces and shrimp. Simmer until hot and add the rice. Let stand until the liquid is absorbed. Serve with a green salad, sour dough bread and a beverage.

Can you imagine? It takes longer to eat it than to prepare. And it's a real treat!

Betty J. Patterson   **Lakewood High School, Lakewood**

Shrimp Creole

¾ onion, chopped
1 clove garlic, pressed or minced
½ cup celery, finely chopped
2 tablespoons butter
1 8 oz. can tomato sauce
½ cup water
1 bay leaf, crushed

1 teaspoon fresh parsley, minced
½ teaspoon salt
1/8 (pinch) cayenne pepper
1 7 oz. package frozen shrimp,
  thawed
1 medium green pepper,
  finely chopped

In medium skillet, saute onion, garlic, green pepper, and celery in butter about 5 minutes or until tender. Remove from heat, stir in tomato sauce, water, bay leaf, parsley, salt, and pepper, simmer 10 minutes. Add additional water, if needed. Add thawed shrimp, bring mixture to boil cook covered over medium flame 5 minutes. Serve shrimp creole over fluffy white rice.

Betty Ann Lawson   **Valencia High School, Placentia**

Shrimp Saute

Serves 2

¼ cup butter
¼ teaspoon Lawry's Garlic Powder
  with Parsley
⅔ to ¾ pound fresh jumbo
  shrimp, with shell

juice of 1 lemon
Lawry's seasoned salt to taste
Lawry's seasoned pepper to taste
parsley, minced (garnish)

Wash, shell (leaving tails attached), devein and butterfly shrimp. In medium skillet, heat butter and garlic powder with parsley; saute shrimp until pink. Add lemon juice, seasoned salt and seasoned pepper. Over high heat, reduce pan juices, remove shrimp to serving plate and add pan juices. Sprinkle with parsley and serve immediately.

This recipe may easily be doubled to serve 4.
A quick, easy and elegant entree.

Lawry's Foods Incorporated   **Los Angeles**

Creamy Fettuccine and Salmon

Serves 6

6 oz. fettuccine
1 lb. salmon steak or fillet*
½ cup dry white wine
1½ pints (3 cups) whipping cream
¼ teaspoon white pepper
1/8 teaspoon nutmeg
10 oz. package Green Giant® sweet peas frozen in butter sauce
3/4 cup parmesan cheese, grated

Cook fettuccine to desired doneness as directed on package; drain. Set aside. In Dutch oven, place salmon in wine; bring to a boil. Reduce heat; simmer covered for 7 to 10 minutes or until salmon is opaque. Lift out salmon; reserve poaching liquid. Discard skin and bones; break into ½ inch pieces. Set aside. Pour poaching liquid through strainer; return strained liquid to Dutch oven. Add cream, pepper, and nutmeg; boil over high heat, stirring occasionally, until reduced to about 2 cups. Add contents of unthawed pea pouch to sauce; simmer over low heat, stirring to separate peas, for 3 to 5 minutes or until peas are thoroughly heated. Add cooked fettuccine stirring gently until thoroughly heated.** Gently fold in salmon. Remove from heat; stir in cheese. Pour onto serving platter.

TIPS:
*One 16 oz. can salmon, drained, boned, and flaked can be substituted for salmon steak. Omit poaching step; add wine with cream to make sauce.

** Additional cream or milk can be stirred in if sauce become to thick.

The Pillsbury Company   **Minneapolis, Minnesota**

Casseroles

Spinach Egg Puff

Serves 6 to 8

10 eggs	1 pint small curd cottage cheese
½ cup flour	1 lb. jack cheese, grated
½ teaspoon salt	½ cup butter, melted
1 teaspoon baking powder	1 package chopped spinach, cooked

Beat eggs with mixer until light. Add rest of ingredients. Pour into well buttered 13x8 inch pyrex dish. Bake at 350° for about 35 minutes.

Ginny Rocheleau   *Muirlands Junior High School, La Jolla*

Eggs Newport

Serves 6 to 8

2 cans cream of mushroom soup	⅓ cup bacon bits
1 cup milk	2 tablespoons chives
1 cup mayonnaise	Small can ripe olives, chopped
12 eggs, hard-cooked	8 strips of bacon, sliced
½ lb. cheddar cheese, grated	ham or Canadian bacon
	6 English muffins

In a bowl, mix together soup, milk and mayonnaise. Set aside. Slice the eggs and place on bottom of 9x13 inch glass dish. Pour sauce over. Sprinkle cheddar cheese over, then layer of bacon bits, chives and ripe olives. Bake at 350° for 30 minutes. to serve, toast English muffins, put bacon strips, ham or Canadian bacon on top and spooon egg casserole over all.

A great brunch dish that can be prepared ahead of time. Serve with a fruit salad and/or vegetable.

Sheryl Malone   *Poway High School, Poway*

Egg Omelette For A Crowd

Serves 12 to 16

butter	6 lbs. bacon, cooked
16 slices white bread	1⅓ cups longhorn cheese, grated
mustard	9 eggs
2 lbs. ham or sausage or	5⅓ cups milk

Butter 8 slices of bread. Put mustard on 8 slices of bread. Cube all the bread into 1½ to 2 inch cubes. Layer ingredients as follows in a 9x13 inch glass pan: buttered bread, ½ of the meat, ⅓ of the cheese, mustard bread, ½ of the meat, ⅓ of the cheese. Beat the eggs, add milk and pour over mixture. Refrigerate overnight. Bake for 30 minutes at 325° (covered). Add ⅓ of the cheese and continue baking (uncovered) for 30 more minutes at 300°.

Perfect for those times when you have house guests and want to make a good impression, but don't want to spend hours in the kitchen. This recipe allows you to cook breakfast while you take your shower, come down a picture of radiant beauty, pop some premade box whole-wheat muffins (containing chopped apples) and glasses of apple juice into the microwave and amaze your guests with a delightful, nutritious breakfast fit for a king. The perfect 'Take It Easy Before Breakfast' menu.

Lois Salisbury   *Mountain View High School, El Monte*

Brunch Eggs

Serves 6

1 cube margarine
1 bunch green onions
1 dozen corn tortillas
8 eggs

1 4 oz. can diced green chilies
1 cup cheddar cheese, grated
1 cup sour cream
6 olives

Melt margarine in electric skillet. Chop green onions and tear tortillas into 2 inch pieces. Saute onions and tortillas in margarine. Beat eggs and chilies together in a bowl. Add eggs to skillet and scramble just till done. Immediately spread grated cheese over top of eggs in skillet. When cheese is melted serve with sour cream. Top with an olive.

Bonnie Parks   *Big Pine High School, Big Pine*

Easy Egg Souffle

Serves 6 to 8

16 slices white bread
butter
1 package cheddar cheese, sliced
1 lb. bacon, fried crispy

6 to 7 eggs, well beaten
1 quart milk
1 teaspoon salt

Trim crust off bread. Butter bread and place 8 slices of the bread, buttered side down in a 9x13 inch pan. Place cheese slices on bread. Top with crumbled bacon. Place the rest of bread on top with the buttered side down. Combine eggs, milk and salt. Pour over bread. Cover and refrigerate overnight. Bake at 350° for 1 hour the next day. Serve with jam or jelly.

Barbara Gauthier   *Santana High School, Santee*

Crustless Artichoke Quiche

Serves 6 to 8

2 green onions, chopped
1 clove garlic, minced
1 tablespoon parsley flakes

2 6 oz. jars artichoke hearts
   (use oil to saute)
5 eggs, slightly beaten
6 soda crackers, crushed
¾ cup cheddar cheese, grated

Saute onion, garlic and parsley flakes in the oil from the artichoke hearts, until tender. Remove from heat and add artichoke hearts, eggs, crackers and cheese. Pour into a 13x9 inch baking dish and bake at 325° for 30 minutes. Cool slightly and cut into squares.

This can be baked ahead of time and reheated.

Katie Morrison-Gold   *Olive Peirce Junior High School, Ramona*

Shepherd Pie

1 can Dinty Moore Beef Stew or
   any canned stew

2 cups Bisquick Mix
⅔ cup milk

Pour the canned stew into a casserole dish. Prepare biscuits with the Bisquick mix and place on top. Bake at 400° for about 20 minutes or until the biscuits are browned on top.

Faye Nielsen   *Rosemead High School, Rosemead*

Quiche Lorraine

Serves 6

1 9 inch pie shell	1 carton whip cream
½ lb. bacon	1 cup half and half
½ lb. Swiss cheese	1/4 teaspoon dry mustard
8 egg yolks	1/8 teaspoon pepper

Bake pie shell 6 to 8 minutes at 425°. Cook bacon until golden and crisp. Drain on towel. Crumble into cooled pie shell. Add Swiss cheese which has been cut in small pieces. Blend egg yolks, whip cream, half and half, dry mustard and pepper. Pour over cheese and bacon. Bake 45 minutes at 350° or until knife comes out clean. Serve hot.

Dorothy Wilson   *Dale Jr. High School, Anaheim*

Mushroom Dill Stroganoff

Serves 4 to 6

2 tablespoons butter	1 cup Knudsen Sour Cream
1 lb. sliced fresh mushrooms	Optional: salt and pepper
⅓ cup dry white wine	Cooked rice or egg noodles
½ teaspoon dry dill weed	

Saute 1 lb. sliced fresh mushrooms in 2 tablespoons butter (in non-stick pan) using medium high heat, stirring constantly for 5 minutes. Add ⅓ cup dry white wine and ½ teaspoon dry dill weed. Stir until liquid cooks down to about 1 tablespoon liquid. Turn heat to low and add 1 cup Knudsen sour cream. Gently stir until heated through. DO NOT ALLOW TO BOIL. Serve immediately over rice or egg noodles for a main dish.

Excellent for vegetarians, but 1 cup cooked beef or turkey can be added with sour cream to increase protein. Before the guests arrive and to save time at the moment of serving dinner, do all the steps (before adding sour cream), then at dinner rewarm mushrooms on low, add room temperature sour cream and heat through.

Ms. Rumenapp   *Santa Monica High School, Santa Monica*

Tuna Noodle Casserole

Serves 4

6 oz. package wide noodles	1 to 1½ cups cheddar cheese,
9½ oz. can tuna	grated
1 can cream of mushroom soup	salt and pepper to taste
¾ can milk or water	paprika or crushed potato chips

Boil noodles 5 minutes, drain. Meanwhile combine tuna, mushroom soup; milk or water, and half of the cheese in greased casserole. Gently fold noodles into soup mixture. Sprinkle remaining cheese over top of noodle mixture. Shake paprika for color or chips for added texture over cheese. Bake 350° for 20 to 30 minutes until cheese bubbles.

Serve with a green frozen vegetable and a tossed salad or relish plate.

Ellie Wildermuth   *La Canada High School, La Canada*

Frittata

Serves 6 to 8

2 tablespoons olive or salad oil
2 tablespoons butter or margarine
½ cup onion, minced
1 cup mushrooms, sliced
vegetables (1 or more): zucchini,
   potato and carrots, shredded;

broccoli, spinach, bean sprouts,
   celery, chopped;
green pepper, minced
6 to 8 eggs
¾ teaspoon salt
cheddar or jack cheese, grated
parsley, chopped

In a large skillet, heat oil and butter, Add onions and mushrooms. Saute 5 minutes. Stir in other vegetables (2 or more cups) and fry lightly. In a small bowl, mix eggs with salt and pour over vegetable mixture in skillet. As eggs set, run a spatula around the edge of skillet, lifting egg mixture to allow uncooked portion to flow underneath. Continue cooking until mixture is almost set. Place skillet under broiler for 1 to 2 minutes or just until top is set. Sprinkle with cheese and parsley. (Can return to broiler for a minute until cheese melts.) Turn onto warm platter. Cut into wedges.

A great way to use up leftovers. Rice or pasta are good additions, or you can add chopped ham, turkey ham, crabmeat, etc. VERY quick and easy AND delicious. Also good cold.

Phyllis Kaylor   **Ray A. Kroc Middle School, San Diego**

California Casserole Picante

Serves 4 to 6

2 cups rice (uncooked)
4 cups tomato juice
1 can mushrooms,
   stems and pieces, drained
1 cup fresh or canned salsa

1 clove garlic, pressed
¼ teaspoon basil (dry)
¼ cup cheddar cheese, shredded
3 tablespoons bread or Italian
   flavored cracker crumbs

Mix everything except ¼ cup shredded cheese and crumbs in a 2 quart casserole dish. Cover mixture with bread crumbs. Top with remaining grated cheese. Bake covered for 45 minutes at 350°, uncovered 10 minutes.

Janet Ballinger   **Las Colinas School, Camarillo**

Broccoli Casserole

Serves 6 to 8

½ cup onions, chopped
6 tablespoons butter
1 10 oz. package frozen broccoli,
   chopped

1 10 oz. can cream of mushroom
   soup
1 8 oz. jar Cheez Whiz
1 cup Minute rice

Saute onions in butter. Add broccoli and simmer until tender. Add remaining ingredients and heat until smooth. Pour into casserole dish and bake ½ hour at 350° or until crust forms on top.

Cathy Smith   **Lone Hill Intermediate School, San Dimas**

Creamy Potato Bake

Serves 6

2 cups water
¾ teaspoon salt
¾ cup milk
2 cups instant potato flakes
1 4 oz. carton whipped
   cream cheese
1 egg beaten

2 tablespoons green onion
   finely chopped
1 tablespoon parsley
   finely snipped
1 tablespoon butter
paprika

Heat 2 cups water and salt to rolling boil in saucepan. Remove from heat. Stir in milk and potato flakes with fork until potatoes are well blended. Add whipped cream cheese; beat well. Stir in beaten egg, chopped green onion and snipped parsley; blend thoroughly. Transfer to a well greased 1 quart baking dish. Dot with 1 tablespoon margarine. Sprinkle lightly with paprika. Bake in hot oven 400° for 30 minutes.

Any leftover regular mashed potatoes may be added to this.

Eleanor Magorien   **El Toro High School, El Toro**

Vegetable Casserole

1 can French cut green beans
1 can whole kernel corn
½ cup onion, chopped
1 can water chestnuts,
   sliced and drained
1 cup mild cheddar cheese, grated

1 can cream of celery soup
1 cup sour cream
1 waxed wrapped package of
   Ritz crackers, crushed
1 stick margarine, melted

Layer in 9x12 inch pan: green beans, corn, onion, water chestnuts and grated cheese. Mix together cream of celery soup and sour cream. Spread over cheese dish. Mix crushed Ritz crackers with melted margarine. Sprinkle cracker mixture over cheese dish. Bake 400° for 40 minutes.

Angie Garrett   **Tenaya Middle School, Fresno**

Chicken and Rice with Almonds

Serves 4

1 cup MJB quick brown rice
4 green onions, chopped
6 medium mushrooms, sliced
1 tablespoon oil
15 almonds, coarsely chopped

¾ cup leftover cooked chicken,
   chopped, OR
1 6 oz. can white meat chicken
1 tablespoon dried parsley
¼ teaspoon pepper
½ teaspoon salt

Prepare rice according to directions on box. Meanwhile in a large skillet saute onions and mushrooms in oil for 2 to 3 minutes. Add almonds, chicken and parsley; stir. Add cooked rice and salt and pepper. Toss well. Heat through for 2 to 3 minutes and serve immediately.

Any leftover cooked rice can be substituted for the brown rice, which can save preparation time. Two teaspoons soy sauce can be substituted for the salt for a more Oriental flavor.

Carol Braun   **Citrus Junior High School, Orange Cove**

Ham and Chicken Casserole

Serves 8

1/4 cup margarine or butter
1/4 cup flour
1/2 teaspoon thyme leaves
1/4 teaspoon salt
1/8 teaspoon pepper
1 16 oz. can chicken broth
1 1/3 cup half and half
3 cups cooked rice

8 oz. (1 1/2 cups) ham, cubed
1 1/2 cups chicken or turkey,
   cubed and cooked
1 10 oz. package frozen peas
   or mixed vegetables
1/4 cup pimento, chopped
1/2 cup slivered almonds or
   toasted almonds

In large saucepan, melt margarine. Stir in flour, thyme, salt and pepper. Cook over low heat, stirring constantly until mixture is smooth and bubbly. Add chicken broth and half and half; cook until mixture boils and thickens, stirring constantly. Stir in remaining ingredients, except almonds. Pour into 3 quart baking dish. Heat in microwave 6 to 10 minutes or until bubbly or bake in 350° oven for 25 minutes. To serve, sprinkle with almonds over baked casserole; garnish with parsley if desired.

Excellent way to use leftover ham, chicken or turkey. Casserole may be prepared ahead and stored in freezer for several weeks.

Mary E. Lash   **Paramount High School, Paramount**

Ham and Broccoli Casserole

2 lbs. tater tots
1 can cream of chicken soup
3/4 cup milk

1/2 cup mayonnaise
1 1/2 cups ham, diced
1 package frozen broccoli
1 cup cheese, shredded

Place tater tots in greased casserole dish. Bake in 350° oven until lightly browned for about 20 minutes. Blend soup with milk and mayonnaise. Stir in ham. Set aside. Place broccoli over browned tater tots. Place ham and soup mixture over broccoli. Sprinkle with cheese. Bake at 350° for 25 to 30 minutes.

This delicious casserole may be made ahead and refrigerated until ready for use.

Bonnie Landin   **Garden Grove High School, Garden Grove**

Party Casserole

Serves 6

3 chicken breasts
1 can cream of chicken soup
2 tablespoons milk
1 cup celery, diced
1/4 cup onion, minced

1 or 2 cans mushrooms, and juice
1 can water chestnuts, diced
1 large can Chinese noodles
1 small jar cashew nuts
jack cheese, grated

Cut boned chicken into bite size pieces. Combine with all ingredients, top with grated cheese. Bake at 350° for 30 minutes.

Great for a luncheon served with fruit or a green salad.

Peggy Himenes   **Actis Junior High School, Bakersfield**

Chicken-Cheese Casserole Ⓜ

Serves 6

2 cups potato chips, crushed
½ cup cheddar cheese, grated
½ cup Swiss cheese, grated
½ cup almonds, chopped
2 cups celery, chopped or
  thinly sliced
1 tablespoon butter

2 cups canned or cooked chicken
  or turkey, chopped
2 teaspoons lemon juice
¼ teaspoon salt
½ cup mayonnaise
2 cups frozen peas, uncooked
½ cup pimento, diced

Combine crushed chips, cheddar cheese and swiss cheese together in a bowl; set aside. Brown nuts and celery in butter. Remove from heat. Stir in chicken, lemon juice, salt, mayonnaise, peas and pimento. Mix thoroughly. Lightly grease a 2 quart casserole. Line bottom with ½ of the cheese-chip mixture. Spoon chicken mixture on top. Top with remaining cheese-chip mixture and bake 350° for 35 to 40 minutes or microwave in covered casserole 6 to 10 minutes.

Additional grated cheese may be added at serving time.

Mary E. Lash   **Paramount High School, Paramount**

Chicken Tetrazine Ⓜ

Serves 6

1 package spaghetti
½ lb. cheddar cheese, grated
½ green pepper, finely chopped
¾ stick margarine
2 cans of mushrooms (save liquid)

2 to 3 cans cream of chicken soup
salt and pepper to taste
3 lbs. chicken or 6 breasts,
  cooked and boned
Salad supreme

Cook spaghetti; drain. Sprinkle with three quarters of the cheddar cheese; set aside. Saute green pepper in margarine and then add drained mushrooms (save liquid). Add chicken soup and chicken. Add mushroom liquid to make soup mixture kind of runny. Season to taste with salt and pepper. Pour over spaghetti into 9x13 inch pan and cover with more cheddar cheese and salad supreme. Reheat at 350° for 45 minutes.

Good way to use leftover chicken or turkey. Can be heated in microwave too!

Carol Christman   **Cerritos High School, Cerritos**

Chicken Enchilada Casserole

Serves 5 to 6

3 chicken breasts,
  cooked and shredded
1 dozen corn tortillas,
  cut in quarters
½ cup onions, minced

1 small can diced Ortega
  green chiles
1 can Campbells cream of chicken
  soup, combined with ½ can water
1½ cups cheddar cheese,
  shredded

Alternately layer tortillas, chicken, onins, chilies, soup and cheese until all ingredients are used. Cover and bake at 350° for 30 minutes.

Sandy Mori   **Alhambra High School, Alhambra**

Chicken Rice Casserole

Serves 6

1 cup raw rice
1 package Lipton onion soup
1 can cream of chicken soup

1 can of water
1 chicken, cut up

Mix first four ingredients and place in a casserole. Top with one cut up chicken. Bake uncovered 350° for 1 hour and 20 minutes.

Roberta S. Priestley   **Alhambra High School, Alhambra**

Tuna-Cheese Biscuit Bake

1 can refrigerator biscuits
1½ cups (10½ oz. can) cheddar
  cheese soup
1 to 2 cans tuna, drained

1 cup milk
2 tablespoons instant minced onion
1 teaspoon parsley flakes

Arrange biscuits in an ungreased 9 inch square baking dish. In a medium mixing bowl combine remaining ingredients; pour over biscuits. Bake 400° for 25 to 30 minutes until biscuits have risen to the top and are well browned. Serve the biscuits with the cheesy sauce spooned on top.

Marie Humphrey   **Grant School, Escondido**

Simple Sausage Casserole

Serves 2

4 sweet Italian sausages
8 to 10 mushrooms, sliced
1 large tomato, sliced
3 green scallions, sliced
½ cup uncooked rice

pinch saffron
½ cup chicken broth
½ cup mushroom soup, undiluted
salt and pepper

Prick sausages and fry until brown. Add mushrooms, tomatoes, scallions, rice and saute 5 minutes. Add saffron, chicken broth, and mushroom soup. *Cover and simmer, stirring occasionally for 20 to 25 minutes or until rice is tender.*

Sandra French   **Long Beach Unified School District**

Italian Hash

Serves 1

2 mild Italian sausage, chopped
1 tomato, chopped
½ onion, chopped
¼ green pepper, chopped
1 baked potato with skin, chopped
½ clove garlic, diced
salt to taste

Fry sausage. Add other ingredients. Cover and simmer 10 minutes. Add water if necessary. Salt to taste.

Joyce Grohmann   **Bellflower High School, Bellflower**

Easy Rellenos

Yields 6

3 cans whole green chiles
3 eggs
1 cup milk
5 tablespoons sifted flour
1 teaspoon oil

10 oz. longhorn cheese,
  cut into 6 strips
*shredded longhorn cheese
  optional
1 cup enchilada sauce

Cut chiles in half lengthwise and remove seeds. Mix eggs and milk in bowl. Add flour and mix well. Add oil and mix. Heat griddle or non-stick skillet over low heat. Place ⅓ cup batter on griddle or in pan and swirl to make 5 to 6 inch circle. Cook until batter firms. Place 1 cheese strip on batter and top with a chile half. Fold sides of batter over cheese and chile. Place in baking dish. When all rellenos are completed, cover with enchilada sauce. Top with generous amount of cheese, if desired, and bake at 350° until heated through and cheese is melted, 10 to 15 minutes.

Cari Sheridan   *Dexter Junior High School, Whittier*

Quick Tamale Pie

Serves 5 to 6

1 lb. lean hamburger
½ onion, diced
1 29 oz. can tomato sauce
2 tablespoons chili powder
1 lb. fresh parsley, snipped

½ teaspoon sage
salt and pepper to taste
1 dozen corn tortillas
½ cup sharp cheddar cheese, grated
1 small can black olives, sliced

Brown hamburger and onion in large skillet. Drain off fat. Add tomato sauce, chili powder, parsley, sage, and salt and pepper and bring to boil. Remove ¾ of sauce from pan. Spread out a layer of corn tortillas over sauce left in pan (about 4 tortillas). Put about ¼ of sauce on top of tortillas — spread it out evenly. Repeat until all sauce and tortillas are used up. Sprinkle top with cheese and black olives. This can be heated on the stove over low heat for 20 minutes — keep covered — or heated in the oven for 30 minutes (covered).

This recipe is easy to increase or decrease as needed.

Carol Stewart   *Barstow High School, Barstow*

Tamale Pie

1 can tamales
1 cup tomatoes, chopped
  (or canned)

1 can whole kernel corn, drained
1 can chili with beans
½ cup cracker crumbs

Break up tamales into bite size pieces. Place at bottom of greased casserole dish. Add tomatoes and corn in layers. Top with chili and beans. Place cracker crumbs on top. Bake 30 minutes at 350°.

This tasty casserole is easy to prepare for those busy days.

Bonnie Landin   *Garden Grove High School, Garden Grove*

Chili Pie

Serves 6 to 8

3 cups Fritos corn chips
1 large onion, chopped

1 cup American cheese, grated

Place 2 cups Fritos corn chips in a 2 quart baking dish. Arrange onion and half the cheese on top. Pour chili over onion and cheese. Top with remaining Fritos corn chips and cheese. Bake at 350° for 15 to 20 minutes.

Antoinette De Neve   *Jones Junior High School, Baldwin Park*

Green Chile Pie

Serves 6 to 8

1 4 oz. can green chiles, chopped
2 cups warm cooked rice
1½ cups jack cheese, grated
2 tablespoons pimiento, chopped

2 tablespoons ripe olives, chopped
  (optional)
6 eggs, slightly beaten
1 teaspoon salt

Combine green chiles, rice, cheese, pimiento and olives. Press into two 8 or 9 inch pie pans to form a crust. Season eggs with salt. Pour over rice mixture. Bake at 350° for 30 minutes or until set. Cut into wedges and serve at once with salad and vegetable.

Deanne Moody   *Monte Vista High School, Spring Valley*

Chili-Cheese Casserole Ⓜ

Serves 6

1 lb. ground beef
1 teaspoon salt
½ teaspoon pepper
¾ cup onion, chopped
1 clove garlic, minced
1 tablespoon chili powder

1 teaspoon paprika
¼ teaspoon oregano
1 8 oz. can tomato sauce
1 l lb. can pinto or kidney beans
1 cup corn chips, crushed
1 cup cheese, grated

Brown seasoned beef and onion; put into a medium casserole. Saute ¼ cup of meat mixture with garlic until golden. Combine all ingredients except chips and cheese. Spoon over hamburger; sprinkle chips and cheese over top. Bake 350° for 30 minutes, or microwave on high power for 10 minutes.

Lou Helen Yergat   *Mission Viejo High School, Mission Viejo*

Joyce's Chili

Serves 4 to 5

1 15 oz. can chili con carne with beans
1 15 oz. can chili con carne without beans
1 lb. hamburger
8 oz. longhorn cheddar cheese (2 cups grated)
1 small bag Fritos

Cook hamburger in skillet until brown. Add the chili and heat with the hamburger meat. Alternate in a casserole, a layer of meat mixture, a layer of grated cheese, and a layer of Fritos. Repeat process until casserole is filled, putting extra Fritos and cheese on top. Place in a 350° oven until cheese melts and Fritos are crisp.

Joyce Grohmann   *Bellflower High School, Bellflower*

Quick Easy Stroganoff

Serves 4

1 lb. hamburger, browned or
1 lb. round steak, sliced thin and
   browned
½ teaspoon garlic salt
1 to 2 teaspoons paprika

1/8 teaspoon black pepper
8 oz. fresh mushrooms, sliced or
   4 oz. can mushrooms
2 cans mushroom gravy
½ cup sour cream or plain yogurt

Mix all ingredients in order given and cook 10 to 15 minutes until flavors blend. Serve over rice or noodles. (To cook rice, use 1 cup rice to 2 cups water.)

Deanne Moody   *Monte Vista High School, Spring Valley*

Hamburger Stroganoff

Serves 4 to 6

1 lb. hamburger
1 tablespoon instant onions,
   soaked in ¼ cup water
1 can cream of mushroom soup

1 teaspoon worcestershire sauce
6 drops tabasco sauce
1/2 teaspoon salt
1/8 teaspoon pepper
cooked rice or toast for serving

Fry hamburger until brown, crumbled. Add instant onions that have been soaked to hydrate. Add soup and spices. Cook over low heat for 10 to 15 minutes. Can add ½ cup water to thin slightly if desired. Serve over cooked rice or toast.

It's so quick, takes so few ingredients, and can be adapted to most situations, casual to formal.

Carol Friesen   *Tehipite Middle School, Fresno*

Easy Beef Stroganoff

Serves 6

1 1 3/8 oz. envelope dry onion
   soup mix
2 tablespoons flour
1/2 cup water

1 4 oz. can mushroom pieces,
   drained
3 cups cooked, dried beef
1 cup sour cream
hot cooked rice

Combine soup mix, flour and water in large skillet. Heat until smooth and thick, stirring constantly. Add mushrooms and beef. Heat. Add sour cream before serving. Serve beef mixture over rice.

Astrid Curfman   *Newcomb Junior High School, Long Beach*

Tater Topped Casserole

Serves 4

½ cup onion, chopped
1 can cream of celery soup,
   undiluted

1 lb. ground round beef
pimentos, (optional)
1 16 oz. pkg. tater tots

Preheat oven to 400°. Grease a shallow 2 quart baking dish. Brown onion and ground round in a skillet. Spoon off fat. Spread in baking dish. Pour soup over meat. If desired, stir in chopped pimentos for garnish. Top with layer of frozen Tater Tots. Bake 35 to 40 minutes or until bubbly.

Cari Sheridan　　　　　　　　　　　*Dexter Jr. High School, Whittier*

Burger Layer "Cake" with Biscuit Bits

Serves 4 to 6

1 egg
1 tablespoon catsup
½ cup bread crumbs
½ teaspoon salt
1 tablespoon worcestershire sauce
1 lb. ground beef
1 can refrigerated biscuits
1 tablespoon margarine

1 teaspoon parsley
2 tablespoons oil
1 onion, diced
½ bell pepper, diced
½ cup corn
1 tomato
¼ teaspoon salt

Combine egg, catsup, bread crumbs, ¾ teaspoon salt and worcestershire sauce. Add meat. Mix well. Divide mixture in half. Shape into two 9 inch patties on a jelly roll pan. Turn oven to 450°. Cut refrigerated biscuits into 4 pieces each. Melt 1 tablespoon margarine in small cake pan. Sprinkle parsley in pan. Coat biscuit pieces with margarine. Bake meat and biscuits 10 mintues at 450°. Saute vegetables 5 to 6 minutes in oil. Add remainder of salt. Sandwich half of the vegetables between meat rounds. Top with remaining vegetables on platter. Place biscuit bits around meat. Serve in hot wedges.

Madelyn V. Fielding　　　　　　　*Jordan High School, Long Beach*

Four Layer Dinner

Serves 4 to 5

3 tablespoons shortening
1 lb. ground beef
¼ teaspoon pepper
1 teaspoon salt
2 teaspoons worcestershire sauce
　or steak sauce

½ teaspoon Tabasco sauce
1 onion, chopped
1 large potato, peeled and
　sliced crosswise
1 green pepper, sliced in rings
1 29 oz. can whole tomatoes

Melt shortening in an electric skillet. Add ground beef and brown. Add pepper, salt, sauces and onion. Spread ground beef mixture evenly over bottom of skillet. Arrange potato slices in a layer over the ground beef. Place green pepper rings on top of potato layer. Pour undrained tomatoes over all. Add water if potato slices are not covered with liquid. Do not mix. Cover; bring to boiling point. Reduce heat and simmer for 40 minutes.

As a girl scout, I got this recipe from a cooking class presented by Southern California Edison Company home economists. It helped me earn a merit badge!

Clyle Alt　　　　　　　　*Bell Gardens High School, Bell Gardens*

Joe's Special

Serves 4

1 10 oz. package chopped frozen
   spinach or broccoli
1 lb. ground beef
1 tablespoon oil

1 small onion, chopped
seasonings to taste:
   salt
   pepper
   oregano
   basil
   marjoram
4 eggs slightly beaten

Thaw spinach or broccoli in strainer. Brown meat and onion in oil; drain.
Add spinach or broccoli and seasonings. Cook until liquid evaporates. Add
eggs to skillet, stir and cook until set.

Penny Niadna　　　　　　　　　　*Golden West High School, Visalia*

Russian Goulash

Serves 4 to 6

1 lb. lean ground beef
1 large onion, diced
1 small green pepper, chopped
1 clove garlic, minced
1 tablespoon paprika
1/2 teaspoon caraway
1 can sliced mushrooms

8 oz. stewed tomatoes with liquid
1 can beef broth or 1 cup bouillon
salt and pepper to taste
8 oz. egg noodles
1/4 to 1/2 cup cooking sherry
sour cream

Brown beef. Add remaining ingredients and simmer 30 minutes. 10 minutes
before serving; add noodles. Just prior to serving, add sherry and top with
sour cream.

Janis Oliver　　　　　　　　　　*Irvine High School, Irvine*

Lee's Meat Loaf

Serves 6 to 8

Meat
2 lbs. ground beef
1 cup oats
1 egg
1 cup milk
1/2 onion, chopped
2 teaspoons salt
pepper
2 teaspoons chili sauce or catsup

Sauce
2 tablespoons worcestershire sauce
2 tablespoons vinegar
1/2 teaspoons paprika
1/2 teaspoon chili powder
1/4 chopped onion
1 cup water
2 tablespoons suger
1 cup catsup

Mix first 8 ingredients together. Place in a large casserole dish. Bake at
400° for 15 minutes. Mix all the sauce ingredients together. Pour over meat
and cook one hour at 350°.

Ginny Rocheleau　　　　　　　*Muirlands Junior High School, La Jolla*

Crusty Crescent Taco Squares

Serves 8

1 lb. ground beef
1/2 cup onion, chopped
1 envelope taco seasoning mix
1 16 oz. can refried beans
1 8 oz. can tomato sauce
2 8 oz. cans refrigerated quick
  crescent dinner rolls
1 tablespoon oil

1/3 cup cornmeal
4 oz. (1 cup) cheddar cheese
  shredded
4 oz. (1 cup) Monterey Jack cheese
  shredded
2 cups lettuce, shredded
1 cup tomatoes, chopped
taco sauce

Heat oven to 375°. Brown meat and onions; drain. Stir in taco seasoning mix, beans and tomato sauce. Simmer 5 minutes. Unroll dough into 4 long rectangles. Place on ungreased 15x10 inch jelly roll pan; press over bottom and 1 inch up sides to form crust. Brush dough with oil; sprinkle with cornmeal. Spoon hot meat mixture over crust. Bake at 375° for 25 to 30 minutes or until crust is golden brown. Sprinkle with cheese. Return to oven until cheese is melted, about 1 to 2 minutes. Cut into squares. Top with lettuce, tomatoes and taco sauce, as desired.

Lynn Robertson   *Esparto High School, Esparto*

Mexican Beef Casserole

Serves 4 to 6

1 lb. ground beef
3 tablespoons minced instant onion
1/2 cup regular white rice
1 15 1/2 oz. can kidney beans,
  undrained

1 16 oz. can stewed tomatoes,
  undrained
1 to 2 teaspoons chili powder
1/2 teaspoon garlic salt
2/3 cup cheddar cheese, grated

Brown meat and drain. Add onion and all remaining ingredients, except cheese. Pour into a greased 2 quart casserole. Cover and bake at 350° for 30 to 35 minutes. Uncover, sprinkle with cheese and bake 10 minutes longer.

Great with some corn and a tossed salad.

Barbara Clark   *El Camino High School, Oceanside*

Tortilla Casserole   Ⓜ

Serves 4

1 lb. lean ground beef
1 tablespoon minced instant onion
1 clove garlic, crushed
2 1/2 teaspoons chili powder
1/2 teaspoon salt
dash of pepper

1/4 teaspoon cumin
2 1/2 teaspoons chili powder
2/3 cup water
1 8 oz. can tomato sauce
1 1/4 cups cheddar cheese, grated

Microwave beef, onion and garlic in covered 2 1/2 quart casserole for 6 minutes. Drain, add chili powder, salt, pepper, cumin, water, tomato sauce and stir. In a round 3 quart casserole dish layer tortillas, meat sauce and cheese, ending with cheese. Cook, covered about 7 minutes on high.

Diane Castro   *Quartz Hill High School, Quartz Hill*

Aunt Edith's Spaghetti

Serves 4

½ to 1 lb. spaghetti noodles,
   broken into 2 inch pieces
½ lb. ground beef
1 medium onion, chopped

6 oz. can tomato paste
12 oz. water
salt, pepper, garlic salt, to taste
parmesan cheese

Boil broken noodles 5 minutes and drain. Brown crumbled ground beef in skillet. Add chopped onions, tomato paste, water and seasonings to beef; simmer with lid on until meat and onions are cooked through. Gently fold in drained noodles until well coated with tomato mixture. Add more water if needed to keep moist. Heat just until hot. Serve with parmesan cheese.

Serve with bread sticks, tossed Italian salad.

Ellie Wildermuth   *La Canada High School, La Canada*

Spanish Noodles

Serves 4

1 medium onion, chopped
1 lb. ground beef
2 cups noodles

2 16 oz. cans of whole tomatoes,
   chopped
¼ cup green pepper, chopped
   (optional)
½ cup chili sauce

Saute onions and ground beef. Add the noodles. Pour chopped tomatoes on top. Sprinkle green pepper on top. Spoon on chili sauce; cover. Bring to boil at 325°. Turn to simmer at 225° and cook 30 to 40 minutes. Stir occasionally.

Barbara Block   *Newport Harbor High School, Newport Beach*

Manicotti with Cheese

Serves 4

6 to 8 manicotti,
   parboiled 3 minutes
8 oz. ricotta cheese
1 egg
¼ lb. mozzarella cheese,
   diced small
1¼ teaspoons chives, chopped fine

1/8 lb. thinly sliced ham,
   diced small
¼ teaspoon salt
dash pepper
1½ to 2 cups spaghetti sauce
   (Paul Newman's or
   Ragu chunky garden style)
grated parmesan cheese

Preheat oven to 375°. Parboil manicotti. In a mixing bowl combine the ricotta cheese, egg, mozzarella cheese, chives, ham, salt and pepper. Mix well. Stuff each piece of manicotti with the cheese mixture. Place the manicotti on a lightly greased shallow pan or casserole. Pour the spaghetti sauce over the manicotti. Sprinkle with grated parmesan cheese. Cover the manicotti with aluminum foil. Bake for 20 minutes. Remove aluminum foil and continue to bake for 15 to 20 minutes or until cheese browns.

Paula Levand   *Canyon High School, Canyon Country*

Mom's Macaroni and Cheese

Serves 4 to 6

2 cups macaroni, uncooked
1 11 oz. can cheddar cheese soup
1 11 oz. can cream of mushroom
 soup

milk (½ of the soup can)
4 tablespoons butter
small onion, chopped
1½ cups cheddar cheese, grated

Put the macaroni in 3 quarts of boiling water to which 1 tablespoon salt has been added. Drain and wash the cooked macaroni in cold water. To this mixture, add the following: cheddar cheese soup, cream of mushroom soup, ½ soup can of milk, chopped onion and 1 cup of cheese. Mix everything together and put into a greased 3 quart casserole dish. Sprinkle with the remaining ½ cup of cheese. Bake at 375° for 30 minutes. Keep covered until the last 10 minutes of cooking.

Don't hesitate to use extra cheese! This was definitely one of my favorites as a child and still is when I go home to vist . . .

Sue Nall   **Temple City High School, Temple City**

Fettucine (Bake) Casserole

Serves 5 to 6

1 box 6 oz. Fettucine Noodle Roni
1 box 10 oz. Birds Eye Broccoli
 with cheese sauce

1 box 10 oz. Birds Eye Cauliflower
 with cheese sauce
¼ cup parmesan cheese

Cook fettucine. Follow directions on the box. Place in a large bowl. Cook broccoli and cauliflower while fettucine is cooking. Follow directions on the box. Place cooked broccoli and cauliflower over fettucine. Add ¼ cup parmesan cheese over fettucine and vegetables and mix thoroughly.

Vegetarians in the family love this recipe. The entire casserole is ready in 20 minutes. Serve with sliced tomatoes. Try it! You'll like it. Non-vegetarians can add a cup of chicken, turkey or ham, cubed.

Tess Osborne   **Columbus Tustin Intermediate School, Tustin**

Mediterranean Pasta

Serves 4 to 6

3 tablespoons butter
¼ cup green onion, chopped
3 leeks, sliced thinly
⅓ cup red bell pepper, chopped
½ lb. fresh mushrooms,
 thinly sliced

1 cup heavy cream
dash nutmeg
salt and pepper
¼ cup grated parmesan cheese
10 to 12 black pitted olives
16 oz. rotelle pasta (curly)

Melt butter in sauce pan, saute onion, leeks and pepper for 1 minute. Add sliced mushrooms, cooking and stirring until mushrooms begin to wilt. Add 1 cup of heavy cream, nutmeg, salt and pepper to taste. Heat until almost boiling; do not boil. Combine with cooked pasta, sprinkle parmesan over mixture, garnish with black olives.

Delicious served with salad and Italian sausage.

Janet Ballinger   **Las Colinas School, Camarillo**

Pasta Primavera

Serves 2 to 3

¼ to ⅓ lb. thin spaghetti,
  fusilli or angel hair pasta
1 medium zucchini, unpeeled
1 cup fresh broccoli flowers
½ cup fresh green beans
3 to 4 green onions
½ red or green bell pepper

2 tablespoons olive oil
2 cloves garlic, pressed
1 tablespoon fresh parsley,
  chopped
1 tablespoon fresh or frozen basil,
  chopped
2 to 3 tablespoons parmesan
  cheese, grated

Fill a large pot with water and start heating for pasta. Add a little oil to water to prevent sticking. While vegetables are cooking, you should cook your pasta 'al dente'. Slice vegetables: zucchini, broccoli, green beans and green onions. Heat olive oil in medium skillet. Add pressed garlic and heat, no more than 1 minute (do not let garlic brown). Add raw vegetables to skillet and cover. Steam for 2 to 3 minutes. Uncover, stir to mix well and add parsley and basil. Cover again and cook until vegetables are done to your taste. It is best if they are still crunchy. When vegetables are ready, season with salt and pepper to taste. Toss with cooked pasta and sprinkle with cheese.

This is an excellent quick meatless dish. However, ham, prosciutto, shrimp, tuna, salmon, etc. may be added during last cooking stage of vegetables. The quantities of vegetables used to not have to be exact. I sometimes add sliced carrots or mushrooms. If you happen to have a bottle of Lawry's milana pasta sprinkle, that may also be added.

Leota Hill   *Saddleback High School, Santa Ana*

Tortilla Hash

Serves 4

6 Old El Paso corn tortillas
2 tablespoons vegetable oil
6 eggs, slightly beaten
1 teaspoon salt

1 10 oz. can Old El Paso mild
  enchilada sauce
1½ cups (6 oz.) Monterey Jack
  or mozzarella cheese
½ cup water
¼ cup sliced onion

Tear tortillas into 1½ inch pieces. Fry tortilla pieces in 1 inch hot oil until crisp and golden. Remove with slotted spoon. Reserve 2 tablespoons oil in skillet; return tortillas to skillet. Stir in eggs and salt. Cook and stir until tortilla pieces are coated and eggs are set. Stir in enchilada sauce, 1 cup cheese, water and half the onion. Simmer uncovered for 15 minutes. Spoon into serving dish. Top with remaining cheese and onion.

Carol Pompa   *Central School, Oroville*

Fettucine Alfredo

Serves 4

2 quarts water
1 teaspoon salt
2 teaspoons oil
8 oz. wide egg noodles, uncooked
¼ cup butter

1¼ cups heavy cream
1¼ cups parmesan cheese
dash of white pepper
dash of nutmeg
parsley

Combine water, salt, and oil in large sauce pan. Bring to full boil. Gradually add noodles. Reduce heat to a slow boil. Cook, uncovered, 8 to 10 minutes, stirring once, until tender. Drain in colander. Return noodles to sauce pan on low heat. Fold in butter until melted. Pour in cream. Sprinkle with parmesan cheese. Fold and stir until cream is partially absorbed and cheese is melted. Add pepper and nutmeg. Garnish with fresh chopped parsley.

Deborah Brown   *Lindhurst High School, Olivehurst*

Stir Fry Cookery

Sweet and Sour Stir Fry

Serves 6

1 5¼ oz. can chunk pineapple
1 tablespoon vegetable oil
1½ tablespoon brown sugar
½ teaspoon soy sauce
1/8 teaspoon white pepper
4 teaspoons cider vinegar
3 tablespoons peanut oil

⅓ cup cauliflower
⅓ cup broccoli
⅓ cup green pepper
⅓ cup Chinese peapods
⅓ cup carrots
⅓ cup water chestnuts, sliced

Sauce: Drain pineapple, reserving ¼ cup juice. Set the pineapple chunks aside. Pour reserved juice into a small bowl and stir in vegetable oil, brown sugar, soy sauce, white pepper, and vinegar. Set aside.

Vegetables: Break apart cauliflower and broccoli into flowerettes. Cut the green pepper into 1 inch pieces. Slice the carrots ½ inch thick. Clean the peapods. Preheat the peanut oil for 1 minute over medium heat in a wok or large frying pan. Add the vegetables. Quick fry for 2 minutes. Add the pineapple chunks and cook for 1 additional minute, until the vegetables are crisp-tender. Pour the sauce over the vegetables. Stir and continue heating for 3 minutes.

Cathy Miller   *Hesperia High School, Hesperia*

Stir Fry Beef and Vegetables

Serves 4

1 lb. lean boneless beef
    (chuck, round, sirloin or
    flank steak)
1 medium onion
2 tablespoons oil
2 cups celery, sliced diagonally

2 cups fresh bean sprouts
1 cup beef broth
¼ cup soy sauce
1 6 oz. can water chestnuts
4 teaspoons cornstarch
2 tablespoons water

Remove fat from beef. Cut beef into thin slices to make strips about 2 inches long and 1/8 inch wide. Cut onion into eighths and separate into layers. Brown beef quickly in hot oil, lifting and turning. Add celery, bean sprouts and onion. Stir fry about 3 minutes until vegetables begin to look transparent. Add broth and soy sauce. Cover and simmer 2 minutes. Add sliced water chestnuts, then cornstarch mixed with water. Stir until sauce thickens and clears. Serve at once over rice.

NOTE: Other vegetables such as green pepper, cauliflower, pea pods, green peas, or green onion may be added to or substituted for those listed in ingredients.

The rice will probably take longer to cook than the preparation of this main dish. This is easy to prepare, delicious, and low in calories! I serve it often.

Doris L. Oitzman   **Victor Valley High School, Victorville**

Chinese Beef Tomato

Serves 4 to 6

1 lb. round steak, partially frozen
2 tablespoons oil
1 clove garlic, crushed
3 medium onions, cut in wedges
1 green pepper, cut in wedges
3 fresh tomatoes, cut in wedges
2 tablespoons cornstarch
1 tablespoon sugar

1 teaspoon salt
3 tablespoons soy sauce
1 cup water
1 cup raw rice simmered with
    2¼ cups water and 1 teaspoon
    salt for 25 minutes or quick
    cooking rice prepared according
    to package instructions

Prepare rice. Cut steak diagonally across the grain into thin pieces. Heat oil in large skillet or wok. Brown the crushed garlic in the hot oil, then remove from skillet. Reduce heat and brown meat in oil in same pan. Cut up and add onion wedges. While meat and onions continue browning, cut and add green pepper strips. Cut and add tomato wedges. Blend together in a small bowl the cornstarch, sugar, salt, soy sauce and water. Push meat and vegetables to sides of wok and add sauce, stirring constantly. When gravy reaches the desired thickness, serve over fluffy rice.

Lorraine Pepper   *Oceanside High School, Oceanside*

Cajun Stir Fry

Serves 4

2 teaspoons cornstarch
1 to 2 teaspoons cayenne pepper
½ cup water
2 teaspoons worcestershire sauce
1 green pepper, sliced in strips
1 red pepper, sliced in strips

2 carrots, sliced diagonally
2 medium zucchini, sliced diagonally
1 onion, sliced
½ lb. kalbase sausage
½ to 1 cup frozen or fresh
    cooked shrimp

Make sure all vegetables are sliced and ready to go before cooking sauce. All vegetables, except the peppers and the kalbase, are sliced on the diagonal bout ¼ inch thick. In a large skillet on medium high, mix the cornstarch, cayenne pepper, water and worcestershire sauce. Cook, stirring until thick and clear. Add vegetables and sausage and cook until almost tender. Stir in the shrimp and finish cooking. Serve with rice pilaf, garlic bread, and fruit salad.

If you cannot find red peppers, increase green peppers and carrots. We serve crushed red pepper flakes or tabasco sauce on the side for added spice. To speed things up, use a food processor on vegetables.

Penny Williamson   *Valhalla High School, El Cajon*

Stir Fry Beef 'n Broccoli

Serves 5

1 1/4 lb. flank steak
3 tablespoons soy sauce
water
2 teaspoons cornstarch
2 teaspoons ground ginger

1 clove garlic, minced
3/4 lb. broccoli
1 tablespoon oil
1 medium onion,
  cut into thin wedges
1 cup bean sprouts

Cut flank steak across grain into thin slices. Mix soy sauce, water (enough to dissolve cornstarch), cornstarch, ginger and garlic. Pour over beef and stir. Set aside. Cut broccoli and flowerettes about 2 inches long. Slice stalk into 1/2 inch slices (broccoli should measure about 2 cups). Heat 2 teaspoons oil over high heat in large nonstick skillet or wok. Add beef and stir fry until browned about 2 minutes. Remove beef to plate. Add remaining oil to skillet. Add broccoli and onion. Cook and stir 2 minutes. Add 2 tablespoons water, reduce heat and cover. Simmer, stirring occasionally, 3 minutes or until broccoli is crisp-tender. Stir in beef and bean sprouts. Cook and stir until beef and bean sprouts are hot. Serve immediately.

Martha Riediger   *Sequoia Junior High School, Simi Valley*

Shredded Beef with Green Peppers

Serves 4

2/3 lb. beef flank steak
Marinade:
  1 1/2 teaspoons rice wine
  1/2 teaspoon salt
  1 tablespoon vegetable oil
  1 tablespoon sesame oil
  1/2 teaspoon baking soda

3 medium green peppers
1/2 cup vegetable oil
1 tablespoon minced fresh
  ginger root
1/3 cup green onions, sliced
1/4 teaspoon sugar
1 teaspoon salt

Using a sharp knife, slice beef across grain and at an angle into thin strips. Combine marinade ingredients in a medium bowl. Add beef shreds, mix well. Let stand about 15 minutes. Slice green peppers into thin strips. Heat 5 tablespoons oil in a wok over high heat 1 minute. Stir fry marinated beef for 10 seconds. Remove beef, draining well over wok and reduce heat to medium. Stir fry ginger root and green onions for 1 minute. Add green pepper shreds, sugar and salt. Stir fry for 2 to 3 minutes. Add cooked beef. Mix well and serve immediately.

I have my students cook this during our Chinese unit and they are surprised how good "Chinese" food can be!

Lou Obermeyer   *Loma Vista Intermediate School, Riverside*

Tomato Beef

Serves 4

Tender strips of beef and crisply cooked vegetables are coated with a curry flavored sauce for this easy Cantonese dish. Serve with steamed rice.

¾ lb. boneless lean beef
1 teaspoons each: cornstarch and soy sauce
1 tablespoon each: dry sherry and water
¼ teaspoon salt
¼ cup salad oil
cooking sauce (recipe follows)
½ teaspoon fresh ginger, minced

1 clove garlic, minced or pressed
2 large stalks celery cut into ¼ inch thick slanting slices
1 medium size onion, cut into wedges with layers separated
1 green pepper, seeded and cut into 1 inch squares
3 medium size tomatoes, each cut into 6 wedges

Cut beef with the grain into 1½ inch wide strips. Cut each strip across the grain into 1/8 inch thick slanting slices. In a small bowl, combine cornstarch, soy, sherry, water, and salt. Add beef, stirring to coat; then stir in 1½ teaspoons of the oil and let stand for 15 minutes.

Meanwhile, prepare cooking sauce and set aside.

Heat a wok or wide frying pan over the heat. When pan is hot, add 2 tablespoons of the oil. When oil is hot, add ginger and garlic and stir once. Add beef mixture and cook, stirring, until meat is browned on outside but still pink inside (about 1½ minutes); remove from pan and set aside.

Add remaining 1½ tablespoons oil to pan. When oil is hot, add celery and onion; cook, stirring, for 1 minute. Add green pepper and continue cooking and stirring for 1 more minute, adding a few drops of water if needed. Add tomatoes and cook, stirring, for 1 more minute.

Return meat to pan. Stir cooking sauce, add to pan, and cook, stirring, until sauce boils and thickens.

Cooking Sauce: In a small bowl, combine 1 tablespoon each: soy sauce, worcestershire, and cornstarch; 3 tablespoons catsup; 1 teaspoon curry powder; and ½ cup water. Stir until blended.

Claudia Henry   *Colfax High School, Colfax*

Stir-Fry Beef and Vegetables

with

Easy Oriental Sauce Mix

Yields about 1 cup

1½ tablespoons Argo or Kingsford's corn starch
1 tablespoon brown sugar, firmly packed
½ teaspoon fresh ginger, minced
¼ teaspoon garlic powder
dash pepper
2 tablespoons soy sauce
1 tablespoons white vinegar
¾ cup cool beef or chicken bouillon or broth
2 tablespoons dry sherry

In 1-pint jar place corn starch, sugar, ginger, garlic and pepper. Add soy sauce and vinegar; shake well. Add bouillon and sherry. Shake before using. Store covered in refrigerator 1 to 2 weeks. Makes about 1 cup.

Stir-Fry Beef and Vegetables: In medium skillet heat 1 tablespoon Mazola corn oil over medium high heat. Add ½ cup broccoli flowerettes and ¼ cup sliced mushrooms; stir fry 1 minute or until tender-crisp. Remove from skillet. Add ¼ pound diagonally sliced beef; stir fry 1 to 2 minutes. Return vegetables to skillet. Add ⅓ cup Easy Oriental Sauce Mix. Stirring constantly bring to boil over medium heat and boil 1 minute. Stir in 4 cherry tomatoes, halved, until heated through. If desired, serve over rice. Makes 1 serving.

Stir-Fry Chicken and Vegetables: Follow recipe for Stir-Fry Beef and Vegetables. Omit beef. Use 1 whole broiler-fryer chicken breast, boned, skinned, cut in thin strips (4 oz.). (2.0)

Note: Sauce Mix may be frozen. Freeze in tightly covered container in ⅓ cup portions. Thaw completely and shake well before using.

Best Foods   *Englewood Cliffs, New Jersey*

Vegetables

Pat's Quick Broccoli Bake

Serves 8 to 10

2 16 oz. cans cream style corn
1 20 oz. package broccoli spears,
   parboiled
cheddar cheese, grated

1 10 oz. package croutons
bacon bits
1 cup milk

Pam or grease 13x9 inch casserole. Spread one 16 oz. can of cream style corn in casserole. Line broccoli over corn. Sprinkle cheese over broccoli then croutons and bacon bits over cheese. Pour milk over top. Spread second can of cream style corn on top. Bake in 350° oven for 45 to 50 minutes.

June Muraoka   *Cypress High School, Cypress*

Corn Casserole

Serves 4

1 can cream corn
2 eggs
2 tablespoons flour
1/2 cup milk

1/2 cup sugar
1/4 teaspoon salt
1/3 cup butter or margarine

Mix all ingredients together, except butter. Pour into buttered casserole dish and dot with butter. Bake at 450° for 45 minutes.

My mother-in-law has served this as a part of Thanksgiving dinner for years. It's always a favorite!

Sheryl Malone   *Poway High School, Poway*

Baby Carrots with Tarragon   Ⓜ

Serves 4

20 oz. package of frozen whole
   baby carrots
1/2 cup water

1/4 cup honey
1 teaspoon tarragon

Place frozen carrots in a pyrex dish with lid. Add 1/2 cup water, 1/4 cup honey and 1 teaspoon tarragon. Cover and put in microwave oven. Cook on high for 20 minutes or until carrots are tender when pricked with a fork.

This is a lovely vegetable served with rack of lamb. Carrots can also be cooked in a regular oven along with lamb.

Nan Paul   *Grant School, Escondido*

Bacon Fried Carrots and Zucchini

Serves 5 to 6

1/2 cup bacon
1 bunch green onions, chopped

6 medium carrots
5 zucchini

Chop bacon and place in frying pan to cook. When bacon begins to cook, add chopped onions (tops and all). Cook until transparent. Wash carrots and cut into thin diagonals. Add to bacon and onions and cook about 4 minutes with lid on pan. Wash zucchini and cut into thin circles. Add to bacon, carrots and onions and cook until carrots and zucchini are tender crisp.

Sue Blass   *Valhalla High School, El Cajon*

Special Green Beans

2 lb. bag or 3 10 oz. packages
   frozen green beans
1 can water chestnuts, sliced
½ cup onion, finely chopped
2 tablespoons margarine

1 teaspoon sugar
1 teaspoon seasoned salt
1 teaspoon vinegar
dash pepper
1 cup sour cream

Cook green beans just until tender. Add water chestnuts and heat through. While beans are cooking, make sauce as follows: saute onion in margarine. Add sugar, seasoned salt, vinegar, pepper, and sour cream. Heat through but do not boil. Serve in a separate dish along side the beans or gently pour over the beans in serving dish.

Delicious with a holiday or very special dinner.

Harriet Trousdale   **Roosevelt Junior High School, Glendale**

Company Vegetable Casserole

Serves 16 to 20

3 1 lb. cans green beans
2 5 oz. cans water chestnuts,
   drained and thinly sliced
2 4 oz. cans mushrooms, drained

2 6 oz. jars artichoke hearts in
   dressing
1 can condensed cream of
   mushroom soup
¼ cup butter, melted

Dump together all of the above (except butter) into a greased 3 quart casserole. Drizzle butter over top. Bake 350° 25 to 30 minutes or until bubbly hot.

This one is good!

Nancy Byrum   **Patrick Henry High School, San Diego**

Stuffed Green Peppers Ⓜ

Serves 6

3 medium green peppers
¾ lb. ground beef
⅓ cup quick cooking rice,
   uncooked
1 teaspoon salt

¼ teaspoon pepper
1 egg
⅓ cup water
1 cup tomato sauce
¼ cup cheddar cheese, grated

Cut green peppers in half, removing core and seeds. Place peppers in 2 quart baking dish. In medium mixing bowl, combine remaining ingredients, using oly half of the tomato sauce. Spoon mixture into pepper halves. Spoon remaining tomato sauce over the meat. Microwave on high speed; (cover with wax paper) 10 minutes or until meat is done.

TIPS: For a softer texture; cook 12 to 13 minutes. ¼ cup grated cheese may be sprinkled on the top and microwaved until melted. The peppers freeze well after being cooked for 10 minutes. Reheat frozen peppers; 3 peppers; 7 minutes, 6 peppers; 10 minutes, 30 seconds.

Bonnie Shrock   **Kearny High School, San Diego**

Mushroom a la Escargot

1/4 lb. margarine
2 garlic cloves, minced
2 tablespoons fresh parsley, minced

2 green onions, minced
2 tablespoons grated
   parmesan cheese
1 lb. fresh mushroom caps

Melt butter in a microwave dish. Add garlic, parsley, onion, and parmesan cheese to butter. Add mushroom caps; stir and cook 4 to 5 minutes until tender.

Serve with hot sourdough bread to catch the drippings.

Maggie Aguirre   *Auburndale Junior High School, Corona*

Marinade Mushrooms

Yields 6

2 1/2 lbs. fresh small mushrooms
1 cube or 1/2 cup margarine
1/4 cup green onions, chopped

2 large bottle Wishbone Italian
   salad dressing
1/2 cup good white wine (optional)

Wash mushrooms and saute in margarine. Drain. Add onions and marinate in dressing and wine (optional) for 1/2 hour to 1 hour before serving.

Best if made the night before. The longer they marinate, the better the mushrooms.

Brenda Burke   *Mt. Whitney High School, Visalia*

Easy Mushroom Tart

Serves 6 to 8

1 8 oz. can refrigerated quick
   crescent rolls
2 cups fresh mushrooms, sliced

1/4 cup butter, melted
1/4 teaspoon marjoram
2 tablespoons grated
   parmesan cheese

Heat oven to 375°. Separate dough into triangles and make into a flat circle on a medium pizza pan or cookie sheet (ungreased). Seal seams and crimp on edge to hold filling. Toss mushrooms with melted butter and arrange on dough. Sprinkle with marjoram and cheese. Bake at 375° for 20 to 25 minutes.

Letitia Ponomareff   *Wangenheim Junior High School, San Diego*

Stuffed Potatoes

Serves 8

4 large potatoes
1/2 cup butter
1/2 cup milk

1 teaspoon salt
1 cup cheddar cheese, grated
1/2 teapoon paprika

Bake potatoes as usual until fork tender. Cut lengthwise and scoop potato out of the potato skin, leaving 1/8 inch of potato on skin. Whip potato with butter, milk, salt and cheese. Fill the potato skins with the potato mixture. Sprinkle with paprika. Reheat in oven 400° for 15 minutes.

These freeze well.

Benti Dick   *Immanual High School, Reedley*

Super Spud

Serves 4

2 baking potatoes, baked
1/4 cup mayonnaise
1 tablespoon mustard

1/4 teaspoon garlic salt
dash pepper
2 frankfurters, sliced diagonally

Cut potatoes in half. Scoop out shells, mash potatoes. Combine mash potatoes with next four ingredients. Fold in frankfurters. Return to shells mounding high. Bake 20 minutes at 350°. Makes a nice light lunch when served with a salad.

These may be prepared ahead, refrigerated and baked later.

Loretta Salau   **Foothill High School, Bakersfield**

Oven Potatoes

Serves 6

6 Idaho potatoes
1/2 cup vegetable oil
paprika

garlic salt
parmesan cheese

Scrub and quarter potatoes. Pour oil in 9x13 inch baking dish. Place quartered potatoes in dish. Turn to coat all sides with oil. Sprinkle generously with paprika, garlic salt and parmesan cheese. Bake at 375° for 1 hour and 15 minutes.

Lois Armstrong   **Sonora High School, La Habra**

Kahlua Candied Yams

Serves 4 to 6

4 medium sized yams
1/4 cup butter or margarine

1/3 cup brown sugar
1/4 cup Kahlua

Boil yams until tender but still very firm. Peel and halve lengthwise. In a heavy frying pan, melt butter and sugar. Add Kahlua, stir and cook for one minute. Add yams and turn until brown on all sides. Cover; reduce heat and cook about 15 minutes. Turn yams over more before serving.

Kathie Baczynski   **Mt. Carmel High School, San Diego**

Green Chiles and Rice

Serves 6

3 cups cooked rice
1 small can chopped green chiles

8 oz. sour cream
1 1/2 cups cheddar cheese, shredded

Mix rice, green chiles, sour cream, and 1 cup of cheese together. Place in lightly greased 2 quart casserole dish. Sprinkle remaining 1/2 cup cheese on top. Bake in 350° oven until bubbly, about 20 minutes.

Excellent with steak, ham or barbecued foods. Good as a change with meatloaf too.

Sue Blass   **Valhalla High School, El Cajon**

Easy Rice Gourmet

Serves 6

1 4 oz. can mushroom
   stems and pieces
1/4 cup butter or margarine
1/2 cup sherry
1 teaspoon parsley flakes

1 1/2 teaspoon season salt (less if
   you want to cut down on salt)
2 teaspoons minced onion (instant)
1/8 teaspoon pepper
1 cup rice
2 cups water

Drain mushrooms, reserving liquid. Saute mushrooms in butter 2 to 3 minutes. Add sherry and seasonings and simmer 5 minutes. Pour rice over mushrooms; add reserved mushroom liquid and water. Cover and cook slowly 25 to 30 minutes.

Mrs. Linda Robinson   **Sinaloa Junior High School, Simi Valley**

Gourmet Rice

Serves 6

2 tablespoons butter
1 tablespoon olive oil
2 medium onions, halved & sliced
10 to 12 fresh mushrooms, sliced

1 cups uncooked rice
1 1/2 cups chicken bouillon
1/4 cup white wine
1/2 bay leaf

Melt butter; add olive oil. Stir in sliced onions and mushrooms. Cook over medium heat 8 to 10 minutes. Add rice; stir and brown lightly. Add remaining ingredients and bring to a boil. Place a tightly fitting lid on pan. Turn heat down to simmer and cook for 20 minutes. Serve hot.

This rice dish has great flavor and makes a good side dish for everything from broiled hamburger patties to shrimp or lobster. My family loves it.

Aletha Hotaling   **Poway High School, Poway**

Mock Wild Rice

Serves 8

1/4 cup butter or margarine
1 1/3 cups packaged precooked rice
1/4 cup onion, chopped
1/2 lb. fresh mushrooms, sliced
1 cup celery, diced
1/4 cup celery leaves, chopped

1 cup canned, sliced water chestnuts
1 1/2 teaspoon salt
dash of pepper
1 cube bouillon
1 1/2 cups boiling water
1/3 cup pecans, chopped

Melt butter in an electric skillet at 150°. Add rice, onion, mushrooms, celery, celery leaves, water chestnuts, salt and pepper. Saute at 220° for 8 to 10 minutes. Dissolve bouillon in boiling water and add to vegetables. Mix to moisten rice. Bring quickly to a boil at 350°. Reduce heat to 210° and simmer for 2 minutes. Fluff rice, add pecans and mix lightly. Cover, turn off heat and allow to stand for 5 minutes until liquid is absorbed.

This is a wonderful accompaniment for nearly any meat, especially chicken or pork. It smells WONDERFUL while cooking.

Harriet Trousdale   **Roosevelt Junior High School, Glendale**

Pilaf

2 tablespoons butter or margarine
⅓ cup rice
⅓ cup vermicelli

2 bouillon cubes
1½ cups boiling water
⅓ cup bulgur

Melt butter in pan at medium heat. Add rice and vermicelli and brown slightly. Put 2 bouillon cubes in 1½ cups boiling water and dissolve. Add this in pan and the bulgur and stir. Cover and simmer for 15 minutes. DO NOT OPEN before the 15 minutes.

Leona Rice   *Ahwahnee Middle School, Fresno*

Spinach and Rice

Serves 6

1 large onion, chopped
¼ cup olive oil
1 cup long grained rice
½ cup tomato sauce
2 cups boiling water

2 bouillon cubes, (optional)
salt and pepper to taste
1 lb. fresh spinach
juice of ½ lemon

In large saucepan saute onions in hot oil until tender. Add rice; saute a few mintues, stirring constantly. Add tomato sauce, water, bouillon cubes, salt and pepper; bring to boil. Add spinach and cover; simmer 20 minutes or until rice is tender. Let stand 10 minutes. Sprinkle lemon juice on top. Serve warm.

Coula Kootsikas   *Woodrow Wilson High School, Long Beach*

Spinach Casserole

2 lbs. frozen chopped spinach,
   defrost and squeeze dry
3 eggs

1 can cream of mushroom soup
8 oz. cheddar cheese, grated
1 cup mayonnaise

Mix all ingredients. Put in 9x13 inch pan. Place in larger pan with water. Bake 350° for 1 hour.

Brenda Umbro   *San Marcos Junior High School, San Marcos*

Easy Spinach Souffle

Serves 6 to 8

¾ cup onion, minced
4 oz. butter
1 cup sour cream
2⅔ cups spinach, drained and
   chopped or 2 packages of

thawed frozen spinach
1¼ teaspoon salt
¼ teaspoon pepper
8 egg yolks

Mince onions and cook in butter until soft. In a large bowl mix the following: sour cream, drained spinach, salt and pepper. Add to the large bowl the softened onion/butter mixture. Blend well. Add the egg yolks to the mixture in the bowl first, checking that the mixture is not too warm. (You don't want to cook the egg yolks.) Mix well. Turn into an 8x8 inch baking dish. Bake at 475° for 20 minutes.

This can be made ahead and refrigerated until baking.

Donna Adams Small   *Santana High School, Santee*

Spinach Casserole

1 package frozen spinach
    cooked with no salt and drained
    (frozen chopped broccoli may be
    substituted)

1 cup cottage cheese
2 eggs
2 cups cheese, grated (any kind)
parmesan cheese
1 tablespoon lemon juice

Place mixed ingredients in well buttered pan. (Sometimes I sprinkle parmesan over the butter.) Bake 45 minutes at 350°. If doubled, bake 1 hour.

Julie Hampton   *Franklin Junior High School, Long Beach*

Stuffed Tomatoes

Serves 4

4 large firm tomatoes
1 package Stouffers spinach
    souffle thawed

seasoned crumbs
parmesan cheese (optional)

Carefully spoon pulp from tomatoes making sure skin of the tomatoes are not torn. Divide the packaged Stouffers spinach souffle into quarters. Stuff tomatoes. Sprinkle with bread crumbs. Place stuffed tomatoes in a casserole dish. Add approximately ½ inch of water. Bake uncovered 350° for 15 mintues. Sprinkle with parmesan cheese.

This is an ideal vegetable dish for your Christmas dinner.

Kathie Baczynski   *Mt. Carmel High School, San Diego*

Zucchini Casserole

Serves 6 to 8

4 medium zucchini,
    sliced ¼ inch thick
4 medium carrots, sliced
½ cup onion, chopped
4 tablespoons margarine

1½ cups herbed stuffing cubes
1 can cream of mushroom soup
½ can sour cream
½ cup water chestnuts, sliced
parmesan cheese

Cook zucchini and carrots until tender. Saute onion in 4 tablespoons margarine until lightly browned. Mix zucchini, carrots, onions, stuffing cubes, soup, sour cream and water chestnuts together. Put in lightly greased casserole. Bake at 350° for 15 minutes. Sprinkle with cheese and cook 15 minutes longer. Serve hot.

Yvonne Lindrum   *Schurr High School, Montebello*

     Recipe for "Creamy Fettucine with Salmon" on page 67 ➡

Vegie-Tuna Platter

	Steaming time:
3 small artichokes, trimmed	30 to 40 minutes
½ lb. small red potatoes	30 to 40 minutes
1½ cups fresh broccoli flowerettes	8 to 10 minutes
1½ cups fresh cauliflower flowerettes	8 to 10 minutes
16 fresh asparagus spears	8 to 10 minutes
1½ cups sliced carrots	3 to 5 minutes
1 large tomato cut in wedges	
2 cans tuna, drained	

Steam all vegies except tomatoes. When vegies are fork-tender, place in a separate container. Pour 2 tablespoons fresh lime marinade (*), chill four hours or overnight, turning vegies occasionally. To serve, arrange vegies and tuna on a platter. Pour remaining marinade over platter.

*Marinade:

¾ cup oil
¼ cup lemon juice
¼ cup parsley, chopped
1 tablespoon fresh chives, chopped

2 teaspoons onion, grated
½ teaspoon cumin seed, crushed
¼ teaspoon dry mustard

Elaine McLaughlin   United Fresh Fruit and Vegetable Association
Washington, D.C.

Fried Rice

Serves 4

3 slices bacon, diced
½ onion, chopped
1 scrambled egg
4 cups cooked white rice

4 teaspoons soy sauce
pepper to taste
3 tablespoons chives, chopped

Brown bacon and onion in frying pan. Scramble egg (easily done in microwave) and chop. Add egg to bacon-onion mixture. Add cooked rice and mix. Season with soy sauce and pepper. Mix until all the rice is coated. Stir in chives. Heat mixture thoroughly and serve.

Cheryl Sakahara   Piute Intermediate School, Lancaster

Desserts

Banana Ice Cream Cups

Serves 4

2 cups vanilla ice cream
½ cup bananas, mashed

4 chocolate ice cream wafers,
crushed

Mash bananas in a small bowl with a fork. Place chocolate wafers between 2 layers of waxpaper and crush with a rolling pin. Mix all ingredients together in a medium size mixing bowl. Serve in a sherbet cup using a salad plate under the sherbet cup. Garnish each with a cherry.

Our 7th grade cooking students make this each semester.

Marianne Traw   *Ball Junior High School, Anaheim*

Chocolate Mousse

Serves 6

6 oz. semi-sweet chocolate
2 tablespoons Kahlua
1 tablespoon orange juice
2 egg yolks

2 eggs
1 teaspoon vanilla extract
¼ cup sugar
1 cup heavy cream

Melt chocolate in the Kahlua and orange juice over very low heat. Set aside. Put the egg yolks and eggs in blender with vanilla and sugar. Blend for 2 minutes at medium speed. Add heavy cream and blend for another 30 seconds. Add the melted chocolate mixture and blend until smooth. Pour into individual small glasses. Refrigerate.

Lou Obermeyer   *Loma Vista Intermediate School, Riverside*

Pineapple Delight

Serves 6 to 8

2 medium cans fruit cocktail
2 6 oz. cans frozen pineapple juice contentrate
1 quart vanilla ice cream

Drain liquid from fruit. Chill fruit. Mix frozen pineapple juice concentrate and fruit together. Layer fruit mix and ice cream alternately in chilled parfait glasses. Place in freezer compartment of refrigerator until ready to serve. Chill about 2 hours.

Keep fruit in frig in the can so extra time is not needed to chill. Quick to make. Quick to serve.

Marie Humphrey   *Grant School, Escondido*

Frozen Fruit Dessert

Serves 10 to 12

2 cups sour cream
¾ cup sugar
2 teaspoons lemon juice
1 banana

1 8 oz. can crushed pineapple
¼ cup maraschino cherries,
chopped
½ cup walnuts, chopped (optional)

Combine sour cream, sugar, and lemon juice. Fold in remaining ingredients. Spoon into paper baking cups in muffin tins. Freeze. Store in freezer bags. They are always ready.

Leota Hill   *Saddleback High School, Santa Ana*

Chocolate Fondue

Serves 6 to 8

3 3 oz. milk chocolate bars
1/2 cup light or heavy cream
Brandy, Rum, Kirsch or Triple Sec to taste, if desired
1/2 teaspoon cinnamon
1/2 teaspoon cloves

Break chocolate bars into pieces. Combine chocolate, cream, liquor, cinnamon and cloves in a saucepan or chafing dish. Stir over low heat until chocolate is melted and smooth. Serve in a chafing dish over low heat. Add more cream or liquor if fondue gets too thick.

Ideas of things to dip: angel food cake squares, ladyfingers, citrus fruit, strawberries, bananas, pineapple, grapes, apple cubes, nuts, pound cake.

Yvonne Lindrum   **Schurr High School, Montebello**

Chocolate Covered Strawberries

Yields approximately 12 to 24

1 12 oz. package semi-sweet chocolate chips
7 tablespoons butter or margarine
1/2 teaspoon vanilla
1 to 2 pints strawberries

Melt chocolate chips in top of double boiler. Add butter and vanilla. Dip strawberries in chocolate, coating all but the tops evenly. Place on wax paper and put in a cool dry place.

These are especially nice if you use strawberries with stems. Strawberries without stems are pretty too, but require more care to dip.

Pam Ford   **Temecula Valley High School, Temecula**

Marshmallow Fudge

Yields 2½ lbs. (approximately 3 dozen)

1½ packages 6 oz. chocolate chips
1/2 cup walnuts, chopped
1/2 7 oz. jar of marshmallow whip
1 cube butter
2¼ cups sugar
1/2 can evaporated milk

Put chocolate chips, walnuts, marshmallow whip and butter in mixing bowl and set aside. Put the sugar and evaporated milk in a saucepan and boil for 8 to 9 minutes. Pour boiling liquid over first mixture and beat until all is melted. Pour mixture into buttered square 9x9x2 inch pan. Refrigerate until firm. Cut into about 1 to 1½ inch squares.

Connie Salvo   **San Gabriel High School, San Gabriel**

Carmel Corn

Yields 4 quarts

1 cup brown sugar
1/2 cup margarine
1/4 cup light corn syrup

1/2 teaspoon baking soda
4 quarts popped popcorn

Combine brown sugar, margarine, and light corn syrup in large sauce pan. Cook on medium high, stirring occasionally, until the mixture reaches the soft boil stage (236°). Add soda immediately, stirring until thoroughly mixed. Pour over popped corn, stirring until each kernel is coated. Turn mixture into 2 ungreased jelly roll pans and bake at 200° for 1 hour, stirring every 15 minutes. Let cool. Store in airtight container.

It's simple enough for the newest cook but tastes better than any commercially prepared product.

Barbara Adams   **Bonita High School, La Verne**

Disappearing Marshmallows

Yield 10

1 teaspoon cinnamon
1/4 cup sugar
1/4 cup melted butter
10 marshmallows

1 can crescent rolls
1 cup powdered sugar
1 teaspoon vanilla
1 to 2 tablespoons milk

Mix cinnamon and sugar together in a small bowl. Melt butter. Dip each marshmallow in butter then in sugar mixture. Set one marshmallow in center of a crescent roll. Roll up and pinch all sides. Bake on cookie sheet at 375° for 10 to 12 minutes. Mix powdered sugar, vanilla and milk for right consistency. Top each roll with glaze.

Ideal recipe for young children to make. They find it fun and they disappear fast.

Jennifer Gierman   **Ball Junior High School, Anaheim**

Fruity Burrito Ⓜ

Serves 6

1 can pie filling
1 package 10 or 12 inch tortillas
shortening or oil

Put a small amount of pie filling down in center of tortilla. Fold tortilla like a burrito. Fry quickly in hot oil or grease until slightly brown. Drain on paper towels. Put on serving dish, then drizzle with glaze.

Glaze:
1 tablespoon butter, softened
1 cup powdered sugar

3/4 teaspoon vanilla
1 to 2 tablespoons hot water

Mix together softened butter, sugar and vanilla. Stir in water, 1 tablespoon at a time, until glaze is of proper consistency.

Can be frozen and reheated later in microwave.

Kim Frost   **Tulare Union High School, Tulare**

Crescent Dough Cream Cheese Pastry

2 cans crescent roll dough
cinnamon and sugar mixture

Filling:
1 8 oz. package cream cheese
1/2 cup sugar
1 teaspoon lemon juice
1 egg yolk
1 small can crushed pinapple,
   well drained

Remove roll dough from can and place on aluminum foil on cookie sheet. Mix ingredients for filling and place half of mixture down the center of dough. Slit both sides of dough into an arrow pattern. Braid sliced dough alternately from side to side. Stick dough slits with egg white and brush or rub egg white on roll when braiding is done. Make a second roll with second can of dough and remaining cream cheese mixture. Bake at 375° for 15 minutes.

Leonda Lines   *Leuzinger High School, Lawndale*

Coffee Bran Kuchen

Serves 6

1 1/4 cups flour
1 1/2 teaspoon baking powder
1/4 teaspoon salt
1/4 teaspoon baking soda
1 teaspoon instant coffee
1/2 cup brown sugar, packed

1/2 cup butter
1/2 cup bran cereal
1 egg, well beaten
1/2 cup buttermillk
1/2 teaspoon cinnamon

Mix and sift flour, baking powder, salt and baking soda; blend in coffee and brown sugar. Cut in butter, reserve 1/2 cup mixture for topping. Add bran to remaining flour mixture; stir in combined egg and buttermilk just until dry ingredients are moistened. Pour into greased 8 inch round cake pan. Add cinnamon to reserved flour mixture. Sprinkle over batter. Bake at 375° for 30 minutes.

I always use whole wheat flour.

Andrea Roberts   *Meadowbrook Middle School, Poway*

Berry Cream Coffee Cake

Serves 6

1 3 oz. package cream cheese
1/4 cup butter
2 cups Bisquick mix
1/3 cup milk
1/2 cup raspberry preserves

Glaze:

1 cup sifted powdered sugar
1 to 2 tablespoons milk
1/2 teaspoon vanilla

Cut cream cheese and butter into Bisquick mix until crumbly. Blend in the 1/3 cup milk. Turn onto floured surface; knead 8 to 10 strokes. On waxed paper, roll dough to 12 x 8 inch rectangle. Turn onto greased baking sheet; remove paper. Spread preserves down center of dough. Make 2 1/2 inch cuts at 1 inch intervals on long sides. Fold strips over filling. Bake in 425° oven for 12 to 15 minutes. Combine sugar, remaining milk and vanilla. Drizzle on top.

Lisa Yancey   *San Clemente High School, San Clemente*

Ridiculous Coffee Cake

Serves 8 or more

1/2 cube margarine
3/4 cup brown sugar
1 small package butterscotch
   pudding (not instant)
1 package Bridgeford frozen rolls
1 cup nuts, chopped

Grease a bundt pan. Melt margarine and combine with sugar. Sprinkle the package of butterscotch pudding in bottom of bundt pan. Lay in package of Bridgeford rolls. Pour in sugar mixture over rolls and sprinkle with nuts. Cover with waxpaper and let rise overnight or until dough rises to top of pan. Bake at 350° for 30 minutes. Turn out. Serve warm.

Frances Greene   *Vista View School, Fountain Valley*

Fruity Fluffy Cheesecake

Serves 8

1 2/3 cups graham cracker crumbs
1/4 cup sugar
1/3 cup softened butter
1 6 oz. package cream cheese
1 pint sour cream

1/2 cup sugar
2 eggs
1/2 jigger Grand Marinier
1 tablespoons lemon juice
1 1/2 to 2 cups sliced fresh fruit
   (peaches, strawberries)

Prepare a graham cracker crust with first 3 ingredients. Use it to line the bottom of 9x3 inch spring form pan. Reserve 2 tablespoons. Combine cream cheese, sour cream, sugar, eggs, Grand Marinier and lemon juice. Whip with electric mixer until creamy. Fold in fresh fruit. Put in spring form pan; sprinkle with a little reserved crumb mixture. Bake in preheated oven 375° for 5 minutes. Chill overnight. Remove sides of pan to serve.

Make ahead. It is an elegant dessert!

Joan Irvine   *Upland High School, Upland*

Pudding Delight

Crust:
   1 cup flour
   1 stick butter
   1/2 to 3/4 cup pecans, chopped

1st Layer
   1 cup sugar
   3 oz. cream cheese
   1/2 container (9 oz.) Cool Whip

2nd Layer
   2 large boxes instant pudding
   3 cups milk

3rd Layer (Top)
   1/2 container (9 oz.) Cool Whip
   Toasted coconut

Crust: Mix ingredients and bake in oblong cake pan for 25 minutes at 350°.
1st Layer: Cream together and spread on cooled crust.
2nd Layer: Mix and chill; spread on top of first layer.
3rd Layer: (Top): Spread remaining Cool Whip on top of 2nd layer and sprinkle with toasted coconut.

This is great!

Marcia Nye   *Woodrow Wilson High School, Long Beach*

Cherry Crunch Delight

1 can 21 oz. cherry pie filling
1 teaspoon lemon juice
1/2 cup nuts

1 stick butter or margarine, melted
1 package white cake mix
whipping cream or vanilla ice cream

Preheat oven to 350°. Spread pie filling in bottom of 9x9 inch pan. Sprinkle with lemon juice. Combine nuts and melted butter with dry cake mix until crumbly and sprinkle over pie filling. Bake for 35 to 40 minutes until browned. Serve with whipped cream or ice cream.

Elaine Shuman   *Oceanside High School, Oceanside*

Minute Tapioca Pudding

3 tablespoons 'minute' tapioca
3 tablespoon sugar
1/8 tablespoon salt
2 cups milk

1 egg yolk
1/2 teaspoon vanilla
1 egg white
2 tablespoons sugar

Mix tapioca, 3 tablespoons sugar, salt, milk and egg yolk in 1½ quart glass casserole. Let stand 5 minutes. Cook tapioca mixture in microwave for 3 minutes on high, uncovered. Stir, then heat 2½ to 3 minutes longer until mixture comes to a full roll. Stir in vanilla and let mixture stand at room temperature while preparing egg white mixture. Beat egg white until foamy, gradually beating in 2 tablespoons sugar, whipping into soft peaks. Fold into hot mixture. Serve warm or chilled.

Mandarin oranges and/or coconut make a good addition with whipped cream on top.

Wilma Reaser   *Hemet Junior High School, Hemet*

Lillian's Pineapple Cake

2 cups flour
1½ cups sugar
1 teaspoon baking soda
¼ cup brown sugar
1 cup nuts, chopped
1 1 lb. 4 oz. can crushed pineapple
  with syrup

Icing:

⅔ cup sugar
½ cup butter
¼ cup milk
½ cup coconut

Combine first six ingredients in a bowl and mix well. Bake 350°F for 35 to 45 minutes in an 8x8 inch pan or 11x7 inch pan.

Icing: Combine sugar, butter and milk in a saucepan. Bring to a boil and simmer 2 minutes. Pour over warm cake; sprinkle with coconut.

Barb Gibbons   *Harbour View School, Huntington Beach*

Dump Cake

Serves 8 to 10

1 can cherry pie filling
1 large can crushed pineapple,
  drained

1 white or yellow cake mix
¾ cup walnuts, chopped
1½ cubes butter, melted

Spread pie filling evenly in a 9x13 inch baking dish. Top with crushed pineapple. Evenly cover with dry cake mix. Sprinkle walnuts and drizzle with butter. Bake at 350° for 50 to 55 minutes. Serve with whipped cream or ice cream.

Wanda Baral   *Crest View School, Huntington Beach*

22 Minute Chocolate Cake

2 cups flour
2 cups sugar
1 teaspoon salt
1 stick margarine
1 cup water
1/2 cup crisco (hard or liquid)

4 1/2 tablespoons cocoa
1/2 cup buttermilk
2 eggs
1 teaspoon baking soda
1 teaspoon vanilla

ICING:

1 stick margarine
4 1/2 tablespoons cocoa

1/3 cup milk
1 lb. powdered sugar
1 cup nuts, chopped

DO NOT USE A MIXER!
Combine flour, sugar and salt in a large bowl. in a sauce pan combine and bring to a boil the margarine, water, shortening, and cocoa. Pour over flour, sugar and salt mixture. Mix well. Combine buttermilk, eggs, soda and vanilla. Add to other mixture and mix well. Pour into 12x18 inch baking sheet, greased and floured. Bake 20 minutes at 400°F. When cake has baked 18 minutes, combine in a sauce pan: margarine, cocoa, milk and bring to a boil; remove from heat. Add powdered sugar, nuts and mix, Pour over hot cake.

Donna Goble   *Almondale School, Littlerock*

Quick Banana Cake

Serves 9

1/2 cup shortening
1 cup sugar
2 eggs
1 cup ripe bananas, mashed

1 1/4 cups sifted flour
3/4 teaspoon soda
1/2 teaspoon salt
1 cup nuts, chopped

Cream shortening and sugar until light. Add eggs; beat well. Stir in bananas. Mix together flour, soda and salt. Add to banana mixture and mix well. Bake in greased 9x9 inch pan 30 to 35 minutes at 350°. Cut in squares and serve warm with whipped cream.

Perfect solution for those over ripe bananas.

Susie Pendleton   *Cerritos High School, Cerritos*

Mandarin Cake

Cake:
1 package yellow cake mix
1 1/4 cup oil
4 eggs
1 can mandarin oranges,
   undrained

Frosting and Filling:

1 3 1/2 oz. instant vanilla pudding
1 large can crushed pineapple,
   undrained
1 8 oz. carton Cool Whip

Mix cake ingredients thoroughly and pour into three 8 inch cake pans. Bake at 350° for 25 minutes. Cool. Beat pudding and pineapple together and fold in thawed Cool Whip. Spread between layers and frost. Refrigerate overnight.

Judy Lindsay   *Lewis Junior High School, San Diego*

Angel and Cherry Cake

Serves 8

1 Angel food cake, cut in cubes
1 #2 can cherry pie filling

1 package instant vanilla pudding
1½ cups milk
1 cup sour cream

Place ½ of cake pieces in bottom of 9x9 inch pan. Reserve ⅓ of cherry pie filling for garnish. Spoon remainder of pie filling over cake. Pat rest of cake on top. Combine pudding mix, milk, and sour cream and beat until smooth. Spoon over cake and garnish with remaining cherries. Chill for 5 hours and serve.

Rita Tayenaka   *Buena Park High School, Buena Park*

Harvest Pumpkin Cake

Yields 1 large loaf

1 yellow cake mix
2 cups pumpkin
1 teaspoon baking soda
1 teaspoon pumpkin pie spice

2 eggs
½ cup water
½ cup chocolate chips
½ cup walnuts, chopped

Mix all ingredients together, except walnuts, until smooth. Grease 9x5x3 inch loaf pan. Chop walnuts and add to batter. Put batter into greased pan. Bake at 350°, 40 to 45 minutes.

Virgie Ponce   *Sanger High School, Sanger*

Cockeyed Cake

Serves 8

1½ cups flour
5 tablespoons oil
1 cup water
1 teaspoon baking soda
1 teaspoon vanilla

1 teaspoon salt
1 tablespoon vinegar
3 tablespoons cocoa
1 cup sugar

Mix all ingredients together in a 9x9x2 inch baking pan. Bake at 350° for 30 minutes. Serve as is.

Monica Carlson   *Yucca Valley Junior High School, Yucca Valley*

Lemon Pudding Bundt Cake

Serves 12

1 yellow or lemon cake mix
2 small package lemon instant pudding
4 eggs
10 oz. lemon-lime carbonated beverage

Preheat oven to 350°. Grease pan. Mix all ingredients together. Bake for 45 to 55 minutes. Serve plain, with whipped cream or ice cream.

Peg Della Zoppa   *Yucca Valley High School, Yucca Valley*

Pound Cake

Serves 18 plus

3 cups sugar
2 cubes margarine, softened
6 eggs
1 teaspoon vanilla

1 teaspoon lemon extract
3 cups flour
½ pint whipping cream,
   unwhipped

Using a beater, mix sugar with 2 cubes softened margarine. Add 6 eggs; beat well. Add vanilla and lemon extract and beat well. Add flour alternately with whipping cream and mix until well blended. Pour into greased tube or bundt cake pan and bake at 325° (do not need to preheat oven) for 1 hour and 40 minutes, or until knife comes out clean. Cake freezes well. Serve plain or with whipped cream and fresh strawberries or peaches.

Nancy Smith   *Dale Junior High School, Anahiem*

Kahlua Chocolate Cake

Serves 10 to 12

1 18.5 oz. package devil's food
   cake mix
4 eggs
1 cup sour cream
1 cup Kahlua

¾ cup vegetable oil
1 6 oz. package semi-sweet
   chocolate chips
powdered sugar (optional)

In large bowl combine cake mix, eggs, sour cream, Kahlua and vegetable oil. Using electric mixer, beat at low speed to blend, then increase speed and beat 3 to 5 minutes at medium-fast speed. Stir in chocolate chips. Pour batter into greased and floured 10 inch bundt pan or tube pan. Bake at 350° for 55 to 60 minutes or until cake tester inserted in center of cake comes out clean. Cool in pan on rack for 30 minutes. Loosen from pan and invert, removing pan. May be dusted with powdered sugar.

Pam Ford   *Temecula Valley High School, Temecula*

Dreamy Applesauce Cupcakes

1 cup margarine, softened
1 cup brown sugar
2 eggs, well beaten
2 cups flour
½ teaspoon salt
1 teaspoon cinnamon

1 teaspoon nutmeg
1 teaspoon baking soda
¾ cup raisins
1 cup walnuts, chopped
1 cup cold applesauce
1 8 oz. package Dream Whip

Cream margarine with sugar. Add eggs and set aside. Sift flour with salt, spices, and baking soda in a separate bowl. Add raisins and nuts. Blend flour mixture alternately with applesauce to sugar and egg mixture. Pour into greased cupcake pans filling cups half full. Bake 375° for 20 minutes. Remove from oven after testing middle of cupcakes with a toothpick for doneness. Cool and serve each cupcake with a spoon of Dream Whip on top.

Chopped dates may be substituted for raisins.

Elda G. Benson   *Corona Junior High School, Corona*

Peanut Butter Pie

Serves 6 to 8

1 8 oz. package cream cheese
½ cup peanut butter
½ cup powdered sugar
1 Choco Cookie Crust

1 12 oz. carton Cool Whip
½ Hershey bar or squre of
   semi-sweet chocolate

Combine cream cheese, peanut butter, powdered sugar and 6 oz. of Cool Whip (½ container). Mix well and pour into a chocolate cookie crust. Cover with plastic wrap and refrigerate overnight. Before serving, cover pie with remaining cool whip. Grate chocolate and sprinkle on top of the pie.

Rebecca Oppen   *Dana Hills High School, Dana Point*

Fresh Strawberry Pie

Serves 6 to 8

1 cup sugar
2 tablespoons cornstarch
pinch of salt

1¾ cup cold water
1 small package strawberry jello
1 pie shell
2½ to 3 boxes strawberries

Mix sugar, cornstarch and salt; add water. Stir over heat until boiling point. Add jello; stir until dissolved. Cool and chill over ice until jello starts to set. Stack berries in pie shell. Pour jello mixture over berries. Allow to set before serving.

Great favorite at ROP Lemon Tree Restaurant.

Pat Storms   *Marysville High School, Marysville*

Petite Cherry Cheesecakes

Yields one dozen cakes

1 8 oz. package cream cheese,
   softened
¼ cup PLUS 2 tablespoons sugar
1 egg

1½ teaspoon lemon juice
½ teaspoon vanilla
12 vanilla wafers
½ can cherry pie filling

Beat together cream cheese, sugar, egg, lemon juice and vanilla until light and fluffy. Line small muffin pans with 12 paper baking cups; place a vanilla wafer in bottom of each. Fill cups ⅔ full with cheese mixture. Bake at 375° for 15 to 20 minutes or just till set. Top each with about 1 tablespoon cherry pie filling; chill. Recipe may be doubled.

This is a recipe I use in class. Very easy.

Gloria Walker   *Casa Roble Fundamental High School, Orangevale*

Chocolate Chip Pudding Cake

Serves 12

1 chocolate cake mix
4 eggs
½ cup oil
1 pint sour cream

¾ of 12 oz. bag of chocolate chips
1 small chocolate instant
   pudding mix

Preheat oven to 350°. Grease bundt pan. Mix all ingredients well in a large bowl. Pour into the bundt pan. Bake 50 to 55 minutes. Remove cake from pan and cool. If desired, sift powdered sugar over top of cake.

Pat Smith   *Kern Valley High School, Lake Isabella*

Peanut Butter Cookies

Yields 2½ dozen

1 cup sugar
1 cup Crunchy peanut butter
1 egg

Set oven at 375°. Measure and combine all ingredients in small mixing bowl, using an electric beater. Very thick! Form into balls. Place on cookie sheet and flatten with fork tongs. Brown in oven 12 to 14 minutes.

Delicious!

Nikki Van Camp   *Poly High School, Riverside*

Lemon Crisps

Yields 2 dozen

1 package Lemon Cake Mix   1 teaspoon lemon peel
½ cup oil   pecan halves (if desired)
2 eggs

Preheat oven to 350°. Combine all ingredients and mix well. Drop from a teaspoon onto an ungreased cookie sheet. If desired, top each cookie with a pecan half. Bake at 350° for 10 to 12 minutes or until golden. Cool on cookie sheet about 1 minute then remove to rack to finish cooling.

Any flavor cake mix may be used if you change the flavoring.

Karen McCord   *Lindsay High School, Lindsay*

Chocolate Yummies

Yields 3 dozen

1 4 oz. box chocolate pudding mix   ⅓ cup milk
2 cups bisquick   1 teaspoon vanilla
½ cup sugar   1 3½ oz. can coconut canned
1 egg   frosting, optional
¼ cup butter, melted   walnut halves, optional

Combine in the order given, except for the optional frosting and walnut halves. Drop by spoonful onto an ungreased cookie sheet. Bake at 350° about 11 to 13 minutes or until set. Cool and decorate with the frosting and walnuts, if desired, or serve plain. They are very rich and delicious both ways.

This is a recipe that I use when asked to contribute cookies at church or meetings because they look fancier than they really are and everyone likes them.

Gwenn Jensen   *Mira Mesa High School, San Diego*

Cookies

1½ cups sticks butter or margarine
¾ cup brown sugar

1½ cups nuts, chopped
1½ packages graham crackers

Combine butter and brown sugar in a medium sized saucepan and boil for 2 minutes. Break graham crackers into small pieces and line up in a jelly roll pan. Pour sugar mixture over graham crackers, evenly distributing nuts. Bake for 10 minutes in 350° oven.

Alcyone Bass   *Hamilton Junior High School, Long Beach*

Forgotten Cookies

2 egg whites
⅔ cup sugar

6 oz. chocolate chips
1 cup chopped pecans

Stiffly beat egg whites. Gradually add the sugar while beating. Fold in the chocolate chips and pecans. Preheat oven to 350°. Grease cookie sheet. Drop by teaspoonfuls onto cookie sheet. As soon as you put them in the oven, turn it OFF. Leave them in the oven for **at least** 2 hours, 20 minutes. **Do not** open the oven until ready to take them out.

I usually make these in the evening and leave them in the oven all night. Then in the morning they're ready.

Sheryl Malone   *Poway High School, Poway*

Chocolate Chip Cheese Squares

2 chocolate chip cookie rolls
2 8 oz. packages cream cheese

1 egg
1 teaspoon vanilla
⅓ cup sugar

Slice one package of cookies and layer on bottom of 9x13 inch greased pan. Mix cream cheese, egg, vanilla, and sugar; spread over cookie dough. Slice remaining package of cookies and top layers in pan. Bake 35 minutes at 350°. Cool and slice into squares.

Freezes well.

Wanda Baral   *Crest View School, Huntington Beach*

Peanut Butter Bars

1½ cups peanuts
8 cups corn flakes
1½ cups sugar

1½ cups light Karo syrup
1 teaspoon vanilla
1½ cups peanut butter

Measure peanuts and corn flakes into a large bowl and set aside. Mix sugar and Karo syrup in heavy saucepan. Heat over medium heat, stirring constantly until mixture comes to a boil. Remove from heat, stir in vanilla and peanut butter. Stir until smooth. Pour over peanuts and corn flakes and stir until all pieces are coated. Press into a buttered 9x13 inch pan and let cool.

Delicious and nutritious

Shirley Marshman   *West Middle School, Downey*

Yummy Chocolate Bars

Yields 3 dozen bars

1 chocolate cake mix
1 stick butter or margarine, melted

¾ cup creamy peanut butter
1 7 or 7½ oz. jar marshmallow creme

Combine melted butter and dry cake mix. Mix until crumbly. Reserve 1½ cups for top of crust. Pat remaining mixture into ungreased 13x9x2 inch pan. Combine peanut butter and marshmallow creme. Spread evenly on crust. Crumble remaining mixture on top. Bake 20 mintues at 350°. Cool and serve.

Joretta Stewart   *Olive Junior High School, Baldwin Park*

Pumpkin Bars

Yields 24 to 48 bars

1 cup flour
1 cup cake flour
2 teaspoons baking powder
1 teaspoon cinnamon
1 teaspoon baking soda
½ teaspoon salt
1 cup cooking oil
2 cups sugar

4 eggs, well beaten
1 cup pumpkin
1 cup walnuts, chopped

Icing:
3 oz. cream cheese
¾ cup butter
1 teaspoon vanilla
1½ cup powdered sugar

Mix all ingredients well. Pour into ungreased jelly roll pan or two 9x13 inch cake pans (one 9x13 inch pan if you want thicker bars). Bake at 325° for 20 to 30 minutes. Cool; cover with icing.
Icing: Cream all ingredients together with an electric beater.

Monica Carlson   *Yucca Valley Junior High School, Yucca Valley*

Chewy Walnut Squares

Yields 16 squares

1 cup brown sugar, firmly packed
1 teaspoon vanilla
1 large egg
½ cup all purpose flour

¼ teaspoon baking soda
¼ teaspoon salt
1 cup walnuts, chopped

Measure brown sugar and vanilla into mixing bowl and add egg. Stir until smooth and well blended. Sift flour with soda and salt. Add first mixture and stir until all of flour is moistened. Fold in walnuts. Turn into 8 inch square pan prepared with waxed paper or aluminum foil lining. Spread with spoon or spatula. Bake at 350° 18 to 20 minutes. Cool in pan. Lift from pan by paper and place on cutting board. Peel off paper and cut into squares with sharp knife.

Jean L. Dempsey   *Santa Paula Union High School, Santa Paula*

Chunky Mini Chip Cookies

Yields 4 dozen

²/₃ cup butter or margarine
1 cup brown sugar, packed
1 egg
1 teaspoon vanilla
1½ cups unsifted all-purpose flour
½ teaspoon baking soda

1¼ cups quick-cooking or
   old-fashioned rolled oats
½ cup raisins
½ cup unsalted peanuts (optional)
¾ cup semi-sweet chocolate
   Mini Chips

Cream butter and brown sugar in large mixing bowl. Beat in egg and vanilla. Blend in flour, baking soda and rolled oats. Stir in remaining ingredients. Roll into 1 inch diameter balls. Place 8 balls 2 inches apart in circular shape on wax paper covered plate or tray in microwave oven. Microwave on high for 1 to 1½ minutes, turning ¼ turn after 1 minute or until cookies are firm but slightly moist. (Do not overcook.) Allow cookies to stand 10 minutes before removing from wax paper onto cooling rack. Repeat with remaining cookies.

Conventional Method: Mix as above. Drop by teaspoonfuls or roll into balls. Place on lightly greased cookie sheets. Bake at 350° for 10 to 12 minutes or until light brown on bottoms. Do not overbake. Cool on wire rack.

Hershey Foods Corporation   *Hershey, Pennsylvania*

Chocolate Slice & Bake Cookies

Yields 4½ dozen

6 tablepoons butter or margarine
6 tablespoons HERSHEY'S Cocoa
1 cup sugar
2 eggs
1 teaspoon vanilla

2 cups unsifted all-purpose flour
2 teaspoons baking powder
½ teaspoon salt
pecan halves (optional)

Place butter or margarine in medium micro-proof bowl; microwave on high (full power) for 45 seconds to 1 minute or until melted. Add cocoa; blend well. Beat in sugar, eggs and vanilla. Add flour, baking powder and salt, beating until smooth. Shape dough into 3 rolls, 1½ inch diameter x 7 inches long. Wrap in wax paper; chill overnight or until firm. Slice rolls into ¼ inch thick slices. Place 8 slices 2 inches apart in circular shape on wax paper covered palte or tray in microwave oven. Top with pecan half, pressing down slightly. Microwave on medium (½ power) for 2 to 2½ minutes (turning ¼ turn after 30 seconds) or until surface is dry, but cookies are soft when touched. Cool on wax paper.

Conventional Method: Melt butter in saucepan; remove from heat. Stir in cocoa until smooth; pour into mixing bowl. Proceed as above. Bake slices on lightly greased cookie sheet at 350° for 8 to 10 minutes or until firm but slightly soft when touched. Cool on wire rack.

Hershey Foods Corporation   *Hershey, Pennsylvania*

Recipes for this picture on pages 116 - 117 ➡

Peanutty Snack Bars

Yields approximately 3 dozen bars

1 cup light corn syrup
½ cup brown sugar, packed
1½ cups chunk style peanut butter
1 teaspoon vanilla
¼ teaspoon salt
1 cup nonfat dry milk powder

1 cup whole bran cereal
1 cup granola cereal
  (crush large lumps)
1 cup raisins
1 cup semi-sweet chocolate
  Mini Chips

Line 13x9 inch pan with wax paper; set aside. In a micro-proof bowl combine corn syrup and sugar. Microwave on high (full power) for 1½ to 2 minutes or until mixture boils. Stir in peanut butter, vanilla and salt. Mix in remaining ingredients except Mini Chips; press into prepared pan. Sprinkle Mini Chips on top. Allow to set 15 minutes; refrigerate until cool. Cut into bars; store covered in refrigerator.

Conventional Method: In heavy saucepan, combine corn syrup and sugar; bring to boil. Remove from heat; stir in peanut butter, vanilla and salt. Proceed as above.

Hershey Foods Corporation   *Hershey, Pennsylvania*

Double Decker Crunch Squares

Yields 16 to 20 squares

1 cup light corn syrup, divided
½ cup smooth peanut butter
1 teaspoon vanilla
1 cup semi-sweet chocolate
  Mini Chips

2 tablespoons butter
2 cups granola, divided
3 cups wheat or corn flakes cereal,
  divided

Combine ½ cup corn syrup and peanut butter in a micro-proof bowl. Microwave on high 1½ to 2 minutes or until boils. Stir well after 1 minute. Add vanilla, 1 cup granola and 1½ cups cereal flakes to mixture; spread in buttred 8 or 9 inch square pan. Combine remaining ½ cup corn syrup. Mini Chips and salt in a micro-proof bowl. Microwave on high 2 to 3 minutes or until boiling; stir after 1 minute. Stir in remaining cereal; spread over peanut butter mixture. Cool slightly and chill before cutting.

Conventional Method: Bring ½ cup corn syrup to boiling in saucepan. Remove from heat; stir peanut butter and vanilla. Add granola and wheat cereal as above; spread in buttered pan. Bring remaining corn syrup to boiling in a saucepan; stir in Mini Chips and butter. Stir constantly over low heat until smooth. Remove from heat and proceed as above.

Hershey Foods Corporation   *Hershey, Pennsylvania*

◀ *Recipe for "Heavenly Chocolate Sundae Cups" on page 118*

Heavenly Chocolate Sundae Cups

Serves 4

1 cup (½ pint) whipping cream, chilled
½ cup chocolate syrup, chilled
1 tablespoon Amaretto di Saronno liqueur
½ cup toasted almonds, finely chopped
1 pint Baskin-Robbins Chocolate Mousse Royale Ice Cream
Chocolate Sauce (below)
¼ cup toasted almonds, coarsely chopped or sliced
stemmed marachino cherries

Combine whipping cream, and chocolate syrup, in a mixing bowl. Beat until mixture holds its shape. Fold in Amaretto and almonds. Divide into four mounded portions on a waxed paper-lined baking sheet, or in saucer, champaign or sherbet glasses. Using the back of a spoon make a depression in the center of each; mound large enough for a scoop of ice cream. Freeze until firm, about 2 or 3 hours. Place a scoop of ice cream in each chocolate cream cup and return to the freezer. To serve, pour warm sauce over ice cream in cups. Sprinkle with ¼ cup toasted almonds and garnish with maraschino cherries.

Chocolate Sauce: Melt 2 tablespoons butter in a saucepan over low heat. Remove from heat and stir in ½ cup sugar and 3 tablespoons unsweetened cocoa. Add 6 tablespoons half and half, blending well. Cook over low heat, stirring constantly, until mixture just begins to boil. Remove from heat and stir in 1 tablespoon Amaretto di Saronno liqueur. Cool slightly. Or, warm ⅔ cup (a 5-ounce pouch) Baskin-Robbins Hot Fudge Topping, remove from heat and stir in 1 tablespoon Amaretto di Saronno liqueur.

Mary King   *Baskin-Robbins Ice Cream*
                         1985 Show off Recipe prize winner

Fresh Lime Cream Fruit Tarts

Serves 8

⅔ cup sugar
¼ cup corn starch
¼ teaspoon salt
1⅔ cups milk
2 eggs, lightly beaten
1½ teaspoons lime rind, grated
1⅓ tablespoons squeezed lime juice
  (about 3 limes)

1 tablespoon butter
1 baked pastry crust
2 nectarines, sliced
1 banana, sliced
½ cup fresh blueberries
½ cup grapes
2 tablespoons corn syrup (optional)

In a medium sauce pan, combine sugar, corn starch, and salt; mix well, gradually stir in milk. Cook over medium heat, stir constantly, until boils and thickens. Boil one minute; remove from heat slowly. Stir hot mixture into beaten eggs. Return to low heat; cool, stirring constantly, for two minutes. Remove; stir in lime rind, lime juice, butter. Pour into prepared pastry shell and cool; then chill. Before serving arrange fruit in decorative pattern on top of pie. Brush fruit with corn syrup to glaze.

Elaine McLaughlin   *United Fresh Fruit and Vegetable Association*
                                      Washington D.C.

Lemon Whipper Snappers

1 package lemon supreme cake mix
2 cups (8 oz.) cool whip
1 egg
powdered sugar

Mix first three ingredients by hand. Drop by teaspoonsful into powdered sugar. Roll into 1 inch balls. Bake at 350° on a greased cookie sheet for 10 to 12 minutes. Cool 10 minutes before removing from the pan.

Makes a chewy yummy cookie.

Gage Jones   South Pasadena High School, South Pasadena

Blender and
Food Processor Cookery

Easy Cheese Cake

Serves 8

8 oz. cream cheese
2 cups milk
1 small instant vanilla pudding

1 graham cracker pie shell
1 can cherry pie filling

Blend cream cheese and milk in a blender. Add the instant pudding. Blend. Pour into graham cracker shell. Let set for 5 minutes. Pour cherry pie filling over top. Chill.

Bonnie Shrock   *Kearny High School, San Diego*

Instant Cheese Cake

Serves 8

2 envelopes gelatin
juice of ½ lemon (2 tablespoons)
thin strip of lemon peel
½ cup hot milk
¼ cup sugar

2 egg yolks
8 oz. package cream cheese
1 heaping cup crushed ice
½ cup whipping cream
1 graham cracker crust
nutmeg or cinnamon (optional)

Into blender jar put the gelatin, lemon juice and peel. Add hot milk, cover and blend on high speed for 40 seconds. Add sugar, egg yolks and cream cheese, cover and blend on high speed for 10 seconds. Add ice and cream and continue to blend for 15 seconds. IMMEDIATELY pour into crumb crust. Sprinkle with nutmeg or cinnamon if desired.

Have everything ready and lined up before starting because it goes fast. Get it out of the blender container ASAP or it will set up in the jar. My favorite cheesecake.

Sandra French   *Long Beach Unified School District*

Cottage Cheese Brunch Cake

Serves 8

1 pint small curd, low fat cottage
   cheese
½ cup sugar
⅓ cup flour

2 medium eggs
1 teaspoon vanilla or
   almond extract
2 tablespoons margarine, melted
1 pastry shell

Whirl cottage cheese in blender until smooth. Add remaining ingredients and blend until smooth. Pour into pie shell. Bake at 350° for 25 to 30 minutes. Cool before serving. May top with berries, peaches, etc.

It's great!

Angie Garrett   *Tenaya Middle School, Fresno*

Summer Fruit Salad Topped Dressing

1 8 oz. package cream cheese,
   softened
¼ cup milk

2 tablespoons honey
¼ teaspoon almond extract

Beat all ingredients in blender until smooth. Serve with variety of fruits, strawberries, watermelon, grapes, nectarines, etc.

Marty Thweatt   *Granite Hills High School, El Cajon*

Mandarin Orange Cake

Serves 10

1 cup sugar
1 cup flour
1 egg
1 teaspoon baking soda

1 can (11 oz.) mandarin oranges,
  with juice
½ teaspoon salt
½ teaspoon vanilla

Mix all ingredients together in a blender for 3 minutes. Pour into a greased and floured pan. Bake 30 to 40 minutes at 350° Pour glaze over hot cake.

GLAZE:

¾ cup brown sugar
3 tablespoons butter
3 tablespoons milk

Bring all glaze ingredients to a boil. Can top with nuts, coconut, and whip cream if you wish.

So good . . . very moist. Takes only a few minutes to put together!

Dorothy Wilson   *Dale Junior High School, Anaheim*

Creamy Fruit Salad

Serves 8 to 10

1 small package vanilla
  instant pudding
1½ cups milk
⅓ cup frozen orange juice
  concentrate
¾ cup sour cream

2 bananas, sliced
1 large can pineapple chunks,
  drained
1 can mandarin oranges, drained
1 small can sliced peaches,
  drained
2 apples, chopped or sliced

In blender place pudding, milk, and orange juice concentrate. Blend until thick and smooth. Fold in sour cream. Add all fruit and serve. Or, chill until ready to serve.

You may serve this with pound cake or by itself. The fruit stays fresh because of acid in the orange juice. Excellent for showers or parties. Looks wonderful and tastes great.

Marsha R. Martin   *Auburndale Junior High School, Corona*

Strawberry Delight

Serves 8

1 small box vanilla wafers, crushed
1 cube butter
1½ cups powdered sugar

2 eggs
2 baskets fresh whole strawberries
1 small carton Cool Whip

Crush vanilla wafers in food processor and line the bottom of a casserole dish. In food processor cream butter, sugar and eggs. Spread on wafers. Slice strawberries and layer over cream. Spread a Cool Whip layer. Sprinkle with crushed wafers and top with a few whole strawberries.

Easy and adored at Pot Lucks!

Janis Oliver   *Irvine High School, Irvine*

Chili Dip (Food Processor)

½ medium onion, quartered
½ green pepper,
  cut into 1 inch pieces
½ lb. raw chuck or round steak,
  cut into 1 inch pieces
½ 10 oz. can tomato and
  green chiles
½ 15 oz. can tomato sauce

½ 13 oz. can kidney beans,
  drained
1 tablespoon chili powder
½ teaspoon salt
dash of pepper
4 black olives, pitted
2 green onions, including tops,
  cut into 1 inch pieces
2 oz. cheddar cheese, well chilled

Steel Blade: Finely chop onion. Remove and set aside. Finely chop green pepper. Add to onion. Chop meat to ground beef consistency. Set aside. In a frypan, brown ground beef. Drain grease. Add onion, green pepper, tomatoes and green chiles, tomato sauce, kidney beans, chili powder, salt and pepper. Simmer for 20 minutes. **Slicing Disc:** While chili is cooking, slice olives. Set aside. **Steel Blade:** Chop green onions. Set aside. **Shredding Disc:** Shred cheddar cheese. Set aside. Top chili with olives, green onions, and cheese before serving. Serve warm over or with tortilla or corn chips.

Phyllis Chutuk   *Oceanside High School, Oceanside*

Spinach Dip

Serves 15

1 to 2 cups sour cream
½ cup onions, minced
1½ cups mayonnaise
1 10 oz. package frozen chopped
  spinach

1 teaspoon salt
½ teaspoon celery salt
½ cup parsley, minced
¼ teaspoon pepper
1/8 teaspoon nutmeg
serve with fresh vegetables

Use a blender or food processor to blend all ingredients. Prepare vegetables ahead and place in ice water. Use a food processor, if available, to slice up the vegetables.

Whenever this recipe is used, the recipe is always wanted.

Charla Rayl   *El Toro High School, El Toro*

Stacki Uppi

Serves 20

rice (1 cup cooked rice per serving)
chicken, diced (5 chicken breasts
  and thighs
gravy (gravy from chicken plus
  2 cans chicken soup)
1 can Chinese noodles
3 tomatoes, diced
½ bunch celery, diced

¾ lb. cheese, grated
more gravy
more noodles
green onions, chopped
1½ large cans crushed pineapple,
  drained
¼ large package toasted coconut
1 6 oz. can peanuts, chopped

Arrange buffet in order of listed ingredients. Guests are to start with item #1 and place on plate, then #2 on top of that, #3 next, and so on. A food processor is a great help in chopping ingredients. It can all be prepared ahead of time.

This recipe is a great ice breaker with your guests because it's such an unusual way of serving. Delicious!

Charla Rayl   *El Toro High School, El Toro*

Hollandaise Sauce/Broccoli

Serves 5 to 6

1½ lbs. fresh broccoli

Hollandaise Sauce:

3 egg yolks
2 tablespoons lemon juice
¼ teaspoon salt

dash cayenne
½ cup hot butter or margarine
melted

Steam broccoli after having trimmed stem ends and splitting heavy stalks. Steam over hot water for 10 minutes or until fork tender and still bright green in color.

Sauce: In blender container combine egg yolks, lemon juice, salt and cayenne. Cover; turn motor on and off. Remove cover; turn motor to high speed and gradually add butter in steady stream. Turn motor off. Serve immediately or keep warm by placing blender container in 2 inches of hot (not boiling) water. Pour over broccoli and serve.

An easy, elegant vegetable dish.

Jeannie Burns   *Los Osos Junior High School, Los Osos*

Liver Paté Normande

Yields: Approximately 3 cups

3 tablespoons butter
1 medium onion, chopped
1 apple, peeled and chopped
1 lb. chicken livers

salt and pepper
1 teaspoon thyme
2 tablespoons brandy, heated slightly
¼ lb. butter

Melt 3 tablespoons butter in pan and saute onion and apple until browned. Remove from pan; set aside. In the same pan, saute livers until brown, seasoning with salt, pepper and thyme. Don't cook for more than 4 minutes. With a match, light the heated brandy, in saucepan, and pour flaming over chicken livers. Add other ingredients and combine well. Cool for 5 to 10 minutes. Cream ¼ lb. butter in a food processor, add liver mixture, puree until smooth. Put in crocks and refrigerate until time to serve.

Pamela Margosan   *Selma High School, Selma*

Chile Rellenos Casserole

Serves 12 to 15

10 eggs
1 pint small curd cottage cheese
1 lb. jack cheese, grated
2 7 oz. cans green Ortega chiles,
   chopped

½ cup flour
1 teaspoon salt
1 teaspoon baking powder
1 cube butter or margarine
1 can 7 oz. green or red chile salsa

Put all ingredients into electric blender in the order given, except butter and salsa. Melt 1 cube butter in 9x13 inch baking pan. Pour the blender mixture into pan; stir. Bake 350° for 30 minutes. After baking, pour 1 7 oz. can green or red chile salsa over top of casserole. Ready to serve!

Carolyn Crum   *Newhart Junior High School, Mission Viejo*

Microwave Cookery

Fudge (Microwave) Ⓜ

1 lb. powdered sugar
½ cup unsweetened cocoa
½ cup milk

½ lb. butter
1 teaspoon vanilla
½ cup chopped nuts

Lightly grease an 8 inch square pan. Set aside. Place powdered sugar and cocoa in a medium sized heat-resistant, non-metallic mixing bowl. Stir to combine. Add milk and butter to sugar cocoa mixture. DO NOT STIR. Heat, uncovered on full power 3 minutes. After cooking, stir just to combine ingredients. Add vanilla and nuts. Stir until blended. Pour into prepared pan and refrigerate for 1 hour before cutting and serving.

Pamela Margosan   **Selma High School, Selma**

Microwave Peanut Brittle Ⓜ

1 cup sugar
½ cup white corn syrup
1 cup roasted peanuts

1 teaspoon butter
1 teaspoon vanilla
1 teaspoon baking soda

Microwave sugar and corn syrup in a 1½ quart covered dish on high 4½ minutes. Add 1 cup roasted peanuts, microwave on high 3 to 5 minutes. Stir in butter and vanilla; microwave on high 1 to 2 minutes. Add baking soda and stir lightly. (It will foam.) Pour on cookie sheet. Cool, break, and enjoy.

Carol Christman   **Cerritos High School, Cerritos**

Aunt Marie's Rocky Road Ⓜ

1½ cups chopped walnuts
16 oz. package miniature
* marshmallows*

18 oz. package chocolate morsels
1 can Eagle Brand sweetened
* condensed milk*

Place chocolate morsels in bottom of a 4 quart bowl. Pour sweetened condensed milk on top. Microwave at 100% power until morsels are melted. Stir. Mix in nuts and marshmallows. Pour onto buttered cookie sheet. Pat into shape with buttered hands. Cool. Cut into squares.

For a special Easter treat shape warm mixture into egg shapes. Cool.

Rhonda Rohde   **Warren High School, Downey**

Microwave Cheesecake Ⓜ

Serves 10 to 12

6 tablespoons butter or margarine
1½ cups graham cracker crumbs
12 oz. cream cheese, softened

⅔ cup sugar
½ pint (1 cup) sour cream
2 teaspoons vanilla
2 eggs

Place butter in a 9 inch pie plate. Microwave, uncovered on high for one minute or until butter melts. Add cracker crumbs and stir to coat. Press mixture evenly over bottom and side of plate. Microwave, uncovered on high for one minute; set aside. In a 2 quart glass bowl beat cream cheese and sugar until well blended. Beat in sour cream, vanilla and eggs; blend well. Cover with waxpaper. Microwave on medium for seven minutes, beating with wire whip every two minutes, or until thickened. Pour mixture gently into prepared crust (or crust may crack). Microwave, uncovered, on Medium for 3 to 6 minutes, rotating plate ¼ turn every 2 minutes. Filling should jiggle slightly in center when gently shaken. Let stand for 20 minutes then cover loosely with waxpaper and refrigerate overnight. Cut into small wedges and serve. Refrigerate any remaining pieces.

Geri Magee   *Marshall Junior High School, Long Beach*

Microwave Stuffed Mushrooms Ⓜ

1 lb large fresh mushrooms   ¼ cup sour cream
3 green onions, sliced   1 8 oz. package cream cheese
1 tablespoon butter or margarine

Wash mushrooms; remove stems from each cap by twisting. Arrange caps, stem side up in 3 quart, 13x9 inch glass baking dish; set aside. Chop stems fine. Place stems, onions and butter in medium glass mixing bowl. Microwave for 3 minutes, on roast, or until onions are tender. Stir in sour cream; add cream cheese. Microwave for 2½ minutes, on roast, or until cream cheese is softened. Stir well. Divide ingredients into four, 6 oz. each, custard cups. Stir ingredients from one of the variations below into each cup. Fill mushroom cups with one of cream cheese mixtures. Microwave for 5 to 6 minutes, on roast, or until hot.

Variations:

Mexican Mushrooms: Add 1 tablespoon chopped green chilies and ¼ cup shredded Monterey Jack cheese to ¼ of basic recipe. Garnish with one strip of pimento.

Italian Mushrooms: Add 3 slices of crisp bacon, crumbled; 5 black olives, chopped; ¼ teaspoon oregano leaves and ¼ teaspoon sweet basil leaves to ¼ of basic recipe. Garnish each mushroom with dried parsley flakes.

French Mushrooms: Add ¼ cup crumbled blue cheese and 1/8 teaspoon tarragon leaves to ¼ of basic recipe. Garnish lightly with tarragon leaves.

Indian Mushrooms: Add 2 tablespoons flaked coconut and ¼ teaspoon curry powder to ¼ basic recipe. Garnish with paprika.

This is great!

Marcia Nye   *Woodrow Wilson High School, Long Beach*

Shrimp and Rice Casserole Ⓜ

Serves 6

3 cups of cooked rice   1 can cream of mushroom soup
½ cup celery, chopped   2 cups cheese, grated
½ cup green pepper, chopped   4 oz. can mushrooms, drained
2 teaspoons onion, minced   ½ teaspoon each of salt and pepper
¼ cup butter   2 4 oz. cans tiny cooked shrimp

In an oblong casserole place the 3 cups of cooked rice on the bottom. In the microwave cook the celery, green pepper, onion and butter for 5 minutes on high. Now add the cream of mushroom soup, the grated cheese and mushrooms and seasonings and shrimp (rinsed and drained). Mix all these ingredients and pour over the rice. Cook 10 minutes on #8.

Very popular with guests.

Jan Friederichsen   *Vista del Rio Junior High School, Anaheim*

Parmesan Potatoes Ⓜ

Serves 4

¼ cup butter (½ stick)
1 lb. russet potatoes, peeled and
  cut into 1 inch cubes
¼ cup parmesan cheese
8 Ritz crackers
1 teaspoon garlic powder

¼ teaspoon salt
½ teaspoon freshly ground pepper
½ teaspoon paprika
3 tablespoons fresh parsley
1 tablespoon parmesan cheese,
  grated

Heat butter on high in microwave in pie plate or au gratin dish just large enough to accommodate potatoes in a single layer, until butter is melted (about 30 seconds). Add potatoes, stirring to coat evenly. Remove with slotted spoon and set aside. Pour off any remaining butter and reserve. Combine parmesan cheese, crackers, garlic powder, salt, pepper and paprika in food processor or blender and process to fine crumbs. Transfer to plastic bag. Add potatoes in batches, shaking to coat evenly. Return potatoes to dish in single layer. Cover with plastic wrap and cook on high for 5 minutes. Add reserved butter and stir potatoes well. cook uncovered on high until potatoes are fork tender about 2 to 3 minutes. Combine parsley and remaining cheese and sprinkle over top. Spear potatoes with toothpicks and serve hot.

Quick appetizer or side dish. Easily adaptable to any number of servings. The topping is especially good on chicken.

Julie Shelburne   **Tulare Union High School, Tulare**

Potato Casserole Ⓜ

Serves 12

2 lbs. frozen hash brown potatoes,
  thawed
½ cup onion, chopped
salt and pepper to taste
½ cup butter or margarine, melted

1 10½ oz. can cream of chicken
  soup
½ pint sour cream
1 small jar of Cheez Whiz
2 cups corn flakes, crushed
¼ cup butter or margarine, melted

Spread potatoes, onion, salt and pepper into a 9x13 inch glass or microwave proof dish. Mix ½ cup margarine, soup, sour cream and Cheez Whiz in a glass or microwave bowl. Heat in microwave until butter is melted. Remove and stir until smooth and pour over potatoes. Melt ¼ cup margarine and combine with corn flakes. Sprinkle over potatoes. Cover lightly with plastic wrap and cook in microwave for 15 minutes on high. Transfer, uncovered to preheated 425° oven for 5 minutes.

I copied this recipe from the radio years ago and have made it many times for company and pot luck dinners. I always get requests for the recipe. I adapted it for the microwave.

Harriet Trousdale   **Roosevelt Junior High School, Glendale**

Tuna Stuffed Potatoes Ⓜ

Serves 4

4 large baking potatoes
¼ cup hot milk
¼ cup sour cream
¼ cup margarine
1 6½ oz. can water packed tuna,
drained

¼ cup green onions, chopped
½ cup cheddar cheese, grated
salt and pepper to taste
additional grated cheese and
green onions for garnish

Bake potatoes in microwave. Cut a large oval piece of skin from the top of each potato and scrape all the potato from the shell into a warm bowl. Mash potatoes with milk, sour cream and margarine. Stir in drained tuna, green onions and cheddar cheese. Season to taste with salt and pepper. Fill potato shells lightly with the mixture — pile high. Garnish with additional grated cheese. Reheat in hot oven or microwave until cheese melts. Top with a few green onions. Serve immediately.

This recipe makes a delicious quick hot dinner. A crisp tossed green salad garnished with tomatoes and croutons is a good accompaniment.

Sharon Turner   *El Dorado High School, Placentia*

Zesty Vegetable Marinade Ⓜ

3 tablespoons red wine vinegar
¼ teaspoon salt
1½ teaspoons basil
¼ teaspoon black pepper

½ teaspoon pimiento
1 green onion, chopped
¼ teaspoon garlic salt
6 tablespoons salad oil

Combine all above ingredients in a small bowl. This makes ½ cup marinade which will cover 2 to 3 cups vegetables.

To Prepare Vegetables:

Select a combination of vegetables: broccoli, carrots, cauliflower, celery, mushrooms, olives, green pepper or artichoke hearts. Wash and cut vegetables into bite sized pieces. The following vegetables need to be blanched. Use a glass measuring cup covered with saran wrap or covered casserole.

For ½ cup of:	Microwave: (on high)
Carrots, cut diagonally	1 to 1½ minutes
Mushrooms, button sized	15 to 30 seconds
Cauliflower, cut in flowerettes	45 seconds to 1 minute
Celery, cut diagonally	45 seconds to 1 minute
Broccoli, cut in flowerettes	45 seconds to 1 minute
Green pepper, cut in pieces	45 seconds to 1 minute

Make marinade and cut vegetables the day before. Pull out to serve the next day. A crisp accompaniment or snack.

Bonnie Plus   *Sanger High School, Sanger*

Grandma's Sausage and Rice Ⓜ
Serves 4 to 6

1 lb. sausage
1 cup onion, chopped
1 cup celery, chopped
1 can cream of mushroom soup

1 can cream of chicken soup
2 soup cans water
1 cup uncooked rice
1 can mushrooms, optional

Brown sausage, chopped onion and celery in skillet. Drain fat. Add both cans of soup, water, uncooked rice and mushrooms. Mix well with spoon and bake in a dutch oven for 1 hour at 350°. Microwave: works great in a microwave. Cook sausage, onion and celery in microwave until pink disappears. Drain grease. Add other ingredients, stir and cook on high for about 15 minutes. Stir 2 or 3 times while cooking.

My family really enjoys this casserole as it is a spicy change from the traditional hamburger dishes and so-o-o easy to make.

Gloria King   **Schurr High School, Montebello**

Sweet-Sour Meat Balls Ⓜ

1 onion, finely chopped
¾ teaspoon seasoned salt
1 10¾ oz. can tomato soup
3 tablespoons lemon juice

¼ cup brown sugar
1 lb. ground beef rolled into
  small balls
1 can 13¼ oz. pineapple chunks,
  drained

Combine onion, seasoned salt, tomato soup, lemon juice and brown sugar in a 9 inch square glass cake pan. Cook in microwave 7 minutes on full power. Stir twice during this time. Place meat balls in this sauce. Spoon some sauce over meat balls. Cook 7 minutes on high. During this time turn the dish once. Add drained pineapple chunks. Heat 1 minute more. Serve with toothpicks.

These meat balls are also good served as a main dish accompanied with cooked rice or whipped potatoes.

Wilma Reaser   **Hemet Jr. High School, Hemet**

Low Calorie Lasagna Ⓜ
Serves 6

1 package frozen chopped spinach
onions, optional
1 lb. ground chuck
1 8 oz. can tomato sauce

garlic salt, parsley flakes,
  sweet basil, to taste
8 oz. cottage cheese
8 fresh mushrooms, sliced
12 oz. mozzarella cheese, grated

Thaw frozen spinach 4 minutes on high. Crumble and cook ground chuck until almost all pink is gone. Onions may be cooked with meat. Mix cooked meat with tomato sauce and spices. Mix drained spinach with cottage cheese. Make four layers in shallow baking dish. (1) Meat and tomato sauce mixture (2) sliced mushrooms (3) two-thirds of mozzarella (4) spinach-cottage cheese mixture. If a probe is used, set for 155°at 50% power; or, cook 12 minutes at 50% power. Cook covered. Remove from oven and sprinkle remaining mozzarella over top. Heat from casserole will melt cheese.

Marilyn Pereira   **Hanford Union High School, Hanford**

Sensational Supper Ⓜ

Serves 4

1 lb ground beef
½ cup onion, chopped
½ teaspoon pepper flakes
1 8 oz. package cream cheese,
    cubed and softened
1 cup egg noodles, cooked

1 6 oz. can tomato paste
½ cup water
½ cup milk
¼ teaspoon garlic salt
¼ teaspoon pepper
¼ cup parmesan cheese, grated

Mix ground beef, onion and pepper flakes in a 2 quart casserole. Microwave at high (100%) until beef loses pink color, 5 to 9 minutes, stirring once to break up beef. Drain. Stir in remaining ingredients except parmesan. Microwave at high (100%) 2 minutes. Reduce power to medium high (70%). Sprinkle with parmesan. Microwave until heated through, 5 to 7 minutes. If using oven other than Sharp Carousel, rotate dish quarter turn every 2 minutes.

Renee Booth   *Hanford High School, Hanford*

Lemon Flavored Chicken Ⓜ in Butter Sauce

Serves 4

6 tablespoons butter or margarine
¼ cup lemon juice
1 tablespoon lemon peel, grated
4 chicken breasts or
    equivalent pieces

dash of salt
dash of pepper
¼ teaspoon marjoram
¼ teaspoon tarragon
1 tablespoon parsley

Microwave butter on high in a large casserole dish for 2 minutes or until melted. Stir in lemon juice and grated lemon peel. Arrange chicken in casserole dish and sprinkle remaining herbs and spices over meat. Cover and microwave on high for 18 minutes.

Peg Della Zoppa   *Yucca Valley High School, Yucca Valley*

Chicken Breast Parmesan Ⓜ

Serves 4

½ cup seasoned fine dry
    bread crumbs
¼ cup grated parmesan cheese
1½ lbs. boneless chicken breasts
1 egg, well beaten

2 tablespoons olive oil
1 8 oz. can tomato sauce
¼ teaspoon oregano
1 cup mozzarella cheese, grated
grated parmesan cheese

Mix the seasoned bread crumbs and the parmesan cheese. Dip the **skinned** boneless chicken in the egg and then in the bread crumb mixture. Heat oil in skillet. Quickly brown the coated chicken. Place chicken in baking dish. Mix the tomato sauce and oregano. Pour over the chicken. Sprinkle mozzarella cheese on top. Cover the dish and cook in the microwave 5 to 8 minutes or until sauce is bubbly and chicken is tender. Sprinkle with parmesan cheese and heat uncovered 30 to 40 seconds more.

Most children seem to love this dish!

Colleen Nelson   *Roosevelt Junior High School, Selma*

Chili-Stuffed Chicken Breasts ⓜ

Serves 8

4 whole chicken breasts,
  split, skinned and boned
  (or 8 half breasts)
6 tablespoons butter
½ cup cheddar cheese, grated
½ cup jack cheese, grated

2 tablespoons green onion, sliced
4 teaspoons green chiles, chopped
¼ cup butter, melted
1 cup cheddar cheese crackers,
  crushed
1½ teaspoon taco seasoning mix

Pound each raw chicken piece to flatten. Combine the 6 tablespoons softened butter with the cheeses, onions and chiles. Place a portion of mixture at one end of each chicken piece. Roll up each piece, tucking in ends to completely enclose filling. Dip each roll in melted butter to cover. Mix together crackers and seasoning mix, then coat with mixture. Arrange rolls in a circle on a baking dish. Cover with waxed paper. Microwave on high 10 to 12 minutes rotating dish ½ turn after 5 minutes until done. Let stand abut 5 minutes before serving.

Marilyn Pereira   *Hanford Union High School, Hanford*

Cornish Hens with Citrus Glaze ⓜ

Serves 4

2 Cornish hens (1½ lbs. each)
1 onion, quartered
1 stalk celery, cut in fourths
1 slice lemon, cut in half
dash paprika
¼ cup butter or margarine

Citrus Sauce:

½ cup sugar
1 egg, slightly beaten
juice of 1 lemon

Rinse cornish hens in cool water and pat dry. Place onion, celery and lemon in body cavities. Place hens, breast side up, in oval micro-proof baking dish with thickest parts near outside of dish. Rub margarine or butter over hens. Sprinkle with paprika. Cook on high (full power) for 15 minutes. Turn hens, breast side down, and baste with pan juices. Cook on high about 7 minutes. Remove dish from oven and prepare citrus sauce as follows: Stir together in glass measure, sugar, egg, and lemon juice until blended. Cook on 50 percent power, 1 to 1½ minutes or until thickens. (Makes about ½ cup) Return dish to oven, turning hens breastside up and brushing with citrus sauce. Cook on 50 percent power about 4 minutes until glaze is set. Total cooking time: 26-30 minutes.

This main dish is a tasty, easy to fix dinner. To complete the meal, serve quick brown rice with herbs, garden vegetable salad, with orange sherbet for dessert. Bon Appetit!

Carolyn Whitham   **Chaffey High School, Ontario**

Oriental Cornish Hen

Serves 2

½ cup soy sauce
½ cup sherry
¼ cup honey
1 garlic clove, finely minced
1 teaspoon fresh ginger, grated

1 cornish game hen, split
    lengthwise (about 1½ lbs.)
fresh parsley, chopped (garnish)
freshly cooked wild rice

Combine first 5 ingredients in shallow 1½ quart glass baking dish. Cover and cook on high 3 minutes. Arrange hen halves in dish breast side down and baste with sauce. Cover and cook on high 4 minutes. Turn halves over and baste with sauce. Cover and cook on high 4 minutes. Let stand until juices run clear when pricked with fork, about 5 to 8 minutes. Garnish with parsley and serve immediately. Accompany with wild rice and sauce.

Pamela Margosan   *Selma High School, Selma*

Chicken Enchilada Casserole Ⓜ

Serves 4 to 6

2½ cups cooked chicken, diced
1 15 oz. can evaporated milk
1 10 oz. can cream of chicken soup
1 1¼ oz. package, or less, taco seasoning mix
1 medium onion, chopped
1 4 oz. can green chiles, chopped and drained
6 corn tortillas, torn in one inch pieces
¾ cup cheddar or longhorn cheese, diced

In a 2 quart casserole combine all ingredients in order listed. Microwave at high for 11 to 13 minutes, rotating dish ½ turn after 5 minutes.

Carol Pompa   *Central School, Oroville*

INDEX

APPETIZERS & BEVERAGES

BLENDER

BREADS

CASSEROLES

CASSEROLES (continued)

CROCK POT

DESSERTS

DESSERTS *(continued)*

FOOD PROCESSOR

MAIN ENTREES *(Beef, Lamb, Pork, and Veal)*

MAIN ENTREES (continued)

MAIN ENTREES (Poultry)

MAIN ENTREES (Seafood)

China Poot's Best Halibut 64
Chopstick Tuna 62
Creamy Fettuccine and Salmon 67
Fillets Elegante 65
Lemon Pepper Fish (Low Fat) 65
Paella California Style 66
Salmon Bake 64
Savory Stuffed Trout 63
Seafood Bean Casserole 63
Seafood-Cheese Bake 63
Shrimp Casserole 62
Shrimp Creole 66
Shrimp Pea Salad 65
Shrimp Saute 66
Spanish Clam Parmesan 62
Wine-Poached Halibut 64

MICROWAVE COOKERY

Aunt Marie's Rocky Road 126
Baby Carrots with Tarragon 94
Chicken Breast Parmesan 131
Chicken-Cheese Casserole 75
Chicken Enchilada Casserole 133
Chicken Tetrazini 75
Chili-Cheese Casserole 78
Chili Dip 3
Chili-Stuffed Chicken Breasts 132
Cornish Hens with Citrus Glaze 132
Fruity Burrito 105
Fudge 126
Grandma's Sausage and Rice 130
Ham and Chicken Casserole 74
Hot Beef Dip 2
Lemon Flavored Chicken In Butter Sauce 131
Low Calorie Lasagna 130
Microwave Cheesecake 126
Microwave Peanut Brittle 126
Microwave Stuffed Mushrooms 127
Oriental Cornish Hen 133
Parmesan Potatoes 128
Pizza Fiesta 29
Potato Casserole 128
"Red Onion" Nachos 8
Sausage Appetizers 31
Savory Stuffed Trout 63
Sensational Supper 131
Shrimp and Rice Casserole 127
Southern Ham and Sweet Potatoes 48
Stuffed Green Peppers 95
Sweet-Sour Meat Balls 130

MICROWAVE COOKERY (continued)

SALADS

SANDWICHES

SOUPS

STIR-FRY COOKERY

VEGETABLES

VEGETABLES *(continued)*

RECIPES FOR PHOTO PAGES

Alphabetized Contributors List

King, Gloria, 3, 130
Schurr HS
Montebello

Kinney, Donna, 14, 38
Laguna JHS
San Luis Obispo

Kootsikas, Coula, 99
Woodrow Wilson HS
Long Beach

LLL

Landin, Bonnie, 37, 74, 77
Garden Grove HS
Garden Grove

Lash, Mary E., 74, 75
Paramount HS
Paramount

Lawson, Betty Ann, 66
Valencia HS
Placentia

Leo, Linda, 36
La Sierra HS
Riverside

Levand, Paula, 83
Canyon HS
Canyon Country

Lindrum, Yvonne, 100, 104
Schurr HS
Montebello

Lindsay, Judy, 109
Lewis JHS
San Diego

Lines, Leonda, 33, 56, 106
Leuzinger HS
Lawndale

Loranger, Ginny, 35, 43
Luther Burbank JHS
Burbank

Lovett, Carol, 43, 44
Ensign Mid. School
Newport Beach

MMM

Magee, Geri, 127
Marshall JHS
Long Beach

Magorien, Eleanor, 22, 73
El Toro HS
El Toro

Malone, Sheryl, 69, 94, 114
Poway HS
Poway

Margosan, Pamela, 124, 126, 133
Selma HS
Selma

Marshman, Shirley, 114
West Mid. School
Downey

Martin, Marsha R., 35, 122
Auburndale JHS
Corona

McCord, Karen, 41, 113
Lindsay HS
Lindsay

McNulty, Beverly, 20
Lindhurst, HS
Olivehurst

Merrill, Beverly, 6
Wangenheim JHS
San Diego

Miller, Cathy, 88
Hesperia HS
Hesperia

Mitchell, Eudora, 13, 57
Norwalk HS
Norwalk

Moody, Deanne, 7, 78, 79
Monte Vista HS
Spring Valley

Moniz, Diana, 41
Rancho Alamitos HS
Garden Grove

Mori, Sandy, 75
Alhambra HS
Alhambra

Morrison-Gold, Katie, 53, 70
Olive Peirce JHS
Ramona

Muraoka, June, 3, 48, 94
Cypress HS
Cypress

Myers, Sharletta Kay, 36, 51
Demille JHS
Long Beach

NNN

Nall, Sue, 2, 84
Temple City HS
Temple City

Neal, Dixie, 14, 15
Granite Hills HS
El Cajon

Nelson, Colleen, 131
T. Roosevelt JHS
Selma

Niadna, Penny, 46, 62, 81
Golden West HS
Visalia

Nielsen, Faye, 20, 70
Rosemead HS
Rosemead

Nye, Marcia, 107, 127
Woodrow Wilson HS
Long Beach

OOO

Obermyer, Lou, 90, 103
Loma Vista Int. School
Riverside

Oitzman, Doris L., 33, 88
Victor Valley HS
Victorville

Oliver, Janis, 81, 122
Irvine HS
Irvine

Oppen, Rebecca, 13, 112
Dana Hills HS
Dana Point

Oravetz, Cheryl A., 38
Hemet HS
Hemet

Osborne, Tess, 3, 65, 84
Columbus-Tustin Int.
Tustin

Oxford, Sally, 13, 20, 47
Monache HS
Porterville

PPP

Palmer, Helene, 63
Crescenta Valley HS
La Crescenta

Patterson, Betty J., 66
Lakewood HS
Lakewood

Parks, Bonnie, 16, 23, 70
Big Pine HS
Big Pine

Paul, Nan, 17, 47, 94
Grant School
Escondido

Pendleton, Susie, 109
Cerritos HS
Cerritos

VVV

Van Camp, Nikki, 113
Poly HS
Riverside

WWW

Walker, Gloria, 8, 59, 112
Casa Roble Fundamental HS
Orangevale

Walls, Millie, 63
El Dorado, HS
Placentia

Whitham, Carolyn, 132
Chaffey HS
Ontario

Wildermuth, Ellie, 47, 71, 83
La Canada HS
La Canada

Williams, Betty M., 49
East Bakersfield HS
Bakersfield

Williamson, Penny, 89
Valhalla HS
El Cajon

Wilson, Dorothy, 54, 71, 122
Dale JHS
Anaheim

Wuesthoff, Gerry, 27
Lexington JHS
Anaheim

YYY

Yancey, Lisa, 106
San Clemente HS
San Clemente

Yackey, George, 2
Santana HS
Santee

Yergot, Lou, 8, 27, 30, 78
Mission Viejo HS
Mission Viejo

Yeutter, Carolyn, 41
Norco HS
Norco